A WAY INTO SCHOLASTICISM

Cascade Companions

The Christian theological tradition provides an embarrassment of riches: from Scripture to modern scholarship, we are blessed with a vast and complex theological inheritance. And yet this feast of traditional riches is too frequently inaccessible to the general reader.

The Cascade Companions series addresses the challenge by publishing books that combine academic rigor with broad appeal and readability. They aim to introduce nonspecialist readers to that vital storehouse of authors, documents, themes, histories, arguments, and movements that comprise this heritage with brief yet compelling volumes.

TITLES IN THIS SERIES:

Reading Paul by Michael J. Gorman

Theology and Culture by D. Stephen Long

Creationism and the Conflict over Evolution by Tatha Wiley

Justpeace Ethics by Jarem T. Sawatsky

Reading Bonhoeffer by Geffrey B. Kelly

Christianity and Politics in America by C. C. Pecknold

Philippians in Context by Joseph H. Hellerman

Reading Revelation Responsibly by Michael J. Gorman

FORTHCOMING TITLES:

The Epistle to the Hebrews in Social-Scientific Perspective by David A. deSilva

Theological Theodicy by Daniel Castelo

iPod, YouTube, Wii Play by D. Brent Laytham

A Way into Scholasticism

A Companion to St. Bonaventure's
The Soul's Journey into God

Peter S. Dillard

CASCADE *Books* • Eugene, Oregon

A WAY INTO SCHOLASTICISM
A Companion to St. Bonaventure's The Soul's Journey into God

Cascade Companions 13

Cascade Books
An Imprint of Wipf and Stock Publishers
199 W. 8th Ave., Suite 3
Eugene, OR 97401

www.wipfandstock.com

ISBN 13: 978-1-60899-771-8

Cataloging-in-Publication data:

Dillard, Peter S.

A way into scholasticism : a companion to St. Bonaventure's The soul's journey into God / Peter S. Dillard.

xii + 216 p. ; 20.5 cm. — Includes bibliographical references and index.

Cascade Companions 13

ISBN 13: 978-1-60899-771-8

1. Bonaventure, Saint, Cardinal, ca. 1217–1274—Theology. I. Title. II. Series.

BX2180.B66 D55 2011

Manufactured in the U.S.A.

To Cynthia R. Nielsen:
Student, Teacher, Colleague, Friend

Contents

Introduction

The present work introduces some perennial issues and characteristic methods of Scholasticism to a contemporary audience. It is especially intended as a useful guide for Catholic seminarians, clergy, brothers and sisters of religious orders, and laypersons interested in learning more about how Scholastic philosophical theology might illuminate what we believe. However, this guide is not limited to my fellow Catholics. It should also appeal to individuals from different Christian faith communities, non-Christian religions, secularists, students at the advanced undergraduate or graduate level, and scholars from all fields who seek a better understanding of the Scholastic contribution to the Catholic intellectual tradition. Hopefully the work will promote greater philosophical literacy and spur others to undertake their own investigations into the matters covered in these pages. By way of preliminary orientation, I would like to say what the work is and what it is not.

I do not presume to offer *the* way into Scholastic philosophical theology, but only *a* way. Alternative approaches— including historical interpretation, intellectual biography, and comparative analysis—are more suitable for some purposes. Our primary purpose is to begin to appreciate Scholastic philosophical theology, not as a history of arcane ideas or a compendium of dead doctrines, but as a living discipline of thinking. To this end, the approach I adopt is that of a critical commentary on a Scholastic classic, *Itinerarium mentis in Deum*, or *The Soul's Journey into God*, by St. Bonaventure of Bagnoregio. I choose this format partly because commentaries have a long and venerable history in Scholasticism: St. Thomas Aquinas, Bl. John Duns Scotus, and St. Bonaventure himself all wrote extensive commentaries on the Sentences of Peter Lombard. Commenting on Bonaventure's masterpiece in plain English with a minimum of technical jargon should thus convey something of the flavor of medieval speculative inquiry without becoming forbiddingly opaque to the contemporary reader.

The Soul's Journey into God is particularly attractive as a primary text because it is relatively short and written in a direct, humble style that makes it highly engaging. Nevertheless, as we shall soon see, beneath this simple veneer lurks a surprising complexity. What initially appears to be merely a devotional tract is, in fact, the articulation of an extremely sophisticated speculative system addressing a number of fundamental questions in epistemology, metaphysics, the philosophy of mind, dogmatic theology, and contemplative mysticism. Consequently, to engage Bonaventure's text at a deep level is to encounter a wealth of fascinating philosophical and theological material. Another advantage of Bonaventure's text is its eclectic nature. The Seraphic Doctor draws upon manifold conceptual resources: Platonic, Neoplatonic, Aristotelian, and the thought of Pseudo-Dionysius the Areopagite. Studying Bonaventure's text therefore exposes the careful reader to a wide variety of perspectives and encourages him/

her to reflect on whether Bonaventure succeeds in combining them into a coherent philosophical theology. Finally, *The Soul's Journey* is readily available in the original Latin and in several excellent English translations, so that it can easily be read in conjunction with my commentary. Still, I shall take care to quote those passages which are directly relevant to whatever issue I am discussing. I will use the translation by Ewert Cousins, occasionally making minor changes in spelling, phrasing, and punctuation so that the text flows better in contemporary English.

My commentary is not a work of Bonaventure scholarship, as I am no Bonaventure scholar. I do not insist that the views I attribute to him are the only interpretations possible. To me they do seem to be the strongest views attributable to him that remain faithful to his text. Sometimes I will bring in ideas which, though not explicitly mentioned by Bonaventure, strike me as offering a natural development of the basic position he is presenting. My justification for such license is that Bonaventure writes not just for his contemporaries but also for the ages, including for us today. Hence if we are to find his speculative system appealing we must be able to understand and motivate it in our own terms. Once the reader has become thoroughly familiar with Bonaventure's treatise, I encourage him/her to question my interpretations by considering whether better ones can be devised.

I will not only expound Bonaventure's views, I will evaluate them. Evaluation is essential to philosophical theology. You can appreciate paintings without painting, poems without composing poetry, and novels without writing them. Yet you cannot appreciate philosophical theology without practicing it. In some instances, I will conclude that the view

Bonaventure outlines can be developed into a prima facie plausible position; in other instances, my verdict will be that the developed position is prima facie vulnerable to a powerful objection. I mean my use of "prima facie" here to be taken seriously. Perhaps I have overlooked some good objection to a position I judge to be plausible. Or perhaps there is a good defense of a position I judge to be vulnerable. An exercise for the reader is to explore these different possibilities in each matter we examine. By doing so, you will then be practicing Scholastic philosophical theology—which is my hope!

Bonaventure distinguishes seven stages of the soul's journey into God, culminating in mystical ecstasy. My commentary will devote a chapter to Bonaventure's Prologue and to each stage, for a total of eight chapters. We shall conclude by asking how our progress in this work relates to the spiritual journey Bonaventure describes. To facilitate further reflection, at the end of most chapters I shall include one or more discussion questions, as well as a bibliography featuring works cited in the text and suggestions for further reading. Where appropriate, I shall supply references to Bonaventure's other writings, the writings of other Scholastic philosopher-theologians, and helpful books and articles from the secondary literature. To aid the reader I have also included a glossary of key terms used in this work.

Let us begin.

ONE

Critical Inquiry and the Desire to Find the Truth

The Prologue to Bonaventure's *The Soul's Journey into God* may strike many contemporary readers as an unpromising way to begin a philosophical treatise, if not downright wrongheaded. Bonaventure reports that in the early fall of 1259 he withdrew to Mount La Verna, where St. Francis of Assisi is believed to have had a mystical vision of a six-winged Seraph with the face of Christ and to have received the stigmata on his hands, feet, and side.[1] Meditating on St. Francis's vision, Bonaventure took the six wings to represent the six levels of illumination leading to the seventh and final stage of ecstatic contemplation, inspiring him to write down his revelation. Bonaventure immediately professes there to be "no other path but through the burning love of the Crucified,"[2]

1. For an account of St. Francis's vision and his stigmata, see House *Francis of Assisi*, 253–56.

2. Bonaventure, *Soul's Journey in God*, 54.

and his introductory remarks are liberally sprinkled with biblical passages. Mystical visions, paranormal phenomena, Jesus Christ, the Bible as the word of God: aren't these the very things that philosophers should *not* take for granted? Even if a philosopher does believe such things, isn't it incumbent upon him/her to promise to provide sound reasons for believing them? Yet in his Prologue Bonaventure makes no such promise. Given this absence, perhaps *The Soul's Journey* is really just a devotional tract for Catholic insiders, a quaint display of Franciscan piety rather than a serious attempt to discover the truth.

Before we consign Bonaventure's text to the limbo of religious ephemera, however, let us look at something else he says: "For no one is in any way disposed for divine contemplation that leads to mystical ecstasy unless like Daniel *he is a man of desires* (Dan 9:23)."[3] Since for Bonaventure divine contemplation leading to mystical ecstasy encompasses the kind of speculative reasoning typical of philosophical theology, this remark may tell us something about Bonaventure's own conception of critical inquiry. What might that be? Before answering this question, let us consider an alternative conception.

It is tempting to think of philosophy as occurring in an emotional vacuum. Beginning with self-evident premises, the philosopher attempts to derive certain conclusions from them using only rationally acceptable procedures. A famous example is René Descartes, who attempts to arrive at an entire system of knowledge based on his inability to doubt his own existence (*cogito ergo sum*) and other "clear

3. Ibid., 55.

and distinct ideas." Possible candidates for self-evident premises are basic conceptual and mathematical truths (e.g., that something can't have and not have a property P simultaneously; that 2+2=4) and observable facts (e.g., that there are various phenomena that we see, hear, smell, taste, or touch, or at least that we seem to experience). Possible candidates for rationally acceptable procedures include deductive reasoning and the non-deductive methods of natural science. Above all, any personal emotions and desires must be set aside in favor of purely rational and dispassionate inquiry into truth. The philosopher also seeks to refute views which are incompatible with the conclusions he/she derives. In extreme versions of this sort of approach, exemplified by Descartes' First Mediation or the *Cartesian Meditations* of Edmund Husserl, the philosopher is even supposed to set aside his/her beliefs about external reality. Descartes announces that he will doubt these beliefs unless and until they are corroborated by reason. Husserl "brackets" or suspends his belief that there is an independently existing world in order to uncover "eidetic essences" allegedly available to pure consciousness.

A novice can be forgiven for finding this approach to philosophy quite baffling. How on earth do you have any idea exactly which conclusions you should try to prove? They can't be conclusions you hope or wish to be true, since hoping and wishing are personal emotions philosophers are supposed to eschew while conducting their investigations. Maybe, like Descartes, you should start with indubitable data, such as *I am now thinking*, and on the basis of equally indubitable intellectual intuitions, such as *So long as I am thinking I exist*, arrive at indubitable conclusions, such as *I now exist*. But there is a problem with this approach as a general strategy.

Many of the potential philosophical conclusions which interest us—for example, whether or not there are moral absolutes, whether or not we are entirely physical beings, whether or not we are immortal, whether or not there is a God who created and sustains us, and so forth—don't follow from indubitable data via indubitable intellectual intuitions on the model of Descartes' *cogito*. If they did then they would be just as indubitable as the fact that I exist so long as I am thinking. Clearly they aren't; indeed, their lack of certainty is what makes these conclusions, whatever they may turn out to be, so interesting to us. Hence if we are to avoid the intellectual equivalent of staring at our own navels indefinitely we must look beyond Descartes' sterile rationalism for some other engine to drive our philosophical quest for significant truth.

It could even be argued that Descartes' project of radical doubt is recklessness verging on insanity. Descartes countenances the legitimate possibility of an evil genius who deceives him into thinking that there is an external world. He then proposes to discover something about which the evil genius could not deceive him and to derive the existence of a benevolent God, mathematics, and the essence of matter as extension. Yet at the outset of his project, Descartes, who is willing to entertain the evil deceiver as a legitimate possibility, oddly doesn't countenance the equally legitimate counter-possibility of there being a jealous and wrathful God who will damn him eternally should he try to rule out the evil genius possibility all by himself without first seeking divine grace through humble prayer! Neither does Descartes entertain the equally legitimate counter-possibility of an alien entelechy that will obliterate him if he tries to rule out the evil genius possibility or the jealous God possibility, nor does

Descartes consider other alterative but equally legitimate counter-possibilities that can be described. Taking any one of these counter-possibilities seriously and trying to rule it out means not ruling out the others. The result is a kind of intellectual paralysis where the philosopher is left isolated on an island of bare reckoning, unable to advance while remaining dismally dissatisfied.[4]

Bonaventure is recommending a radically different conception of critical inquiry. He fully recognizes that we are emotional creatures. We have hopes, fears, and desires; and we feel strongly about a number of different topics. It is because we are emotionally and even viscerally attracted to certain positions and repelled by others that we argue the way we do, a fact that applies no less to the atheist than it does to the Catholic philosopher-theologian. So, Bonaventure suggests, start there. Start with what you strongly believe and try to find the best reasons you can for it and the best reasons you can against contrary positions. Does that mean everything is subordinated to our feelings? No. Bonaventure emphasizes the importance of being a man or woman of *desires*. I may desire to associate myself with certain views and to dissociate myself from others. I might desire to make a name for myself by devising clever arguments or to discredit those thinkers with whom I disagree. Fortunately, I can also have a deeper desire that orders and disciplines what would otherwise be an unruly, emotional subjectivism: the desire to find the truth. Something isn't true simply because I want it to be. If

---

4. We might christen this predicament "Pascal's Revenge" after the French philosopher-theologian Blaise Pascal, whose famous "wager" or probabilistic argument in support of God's existence is somewhat different from the dilemma described above.

I sincerely desire to find and understand the truth, and if I temper my desire with humility, then I must be prepared to admit that something I believe to be true really isn't, or at least that I have no good reason for believing it to be true. I might also learn that something I believed to be false really isn't, or at least that I have no good reason for denying it. In other cases, a fair amount of reflection may leave me unable to commit myself for or against the belief in question, so that I remain agnostic pending further, more decisive considerations. Whatever the outcome, on Bonaventure's approach it is the desire to find and understand the truth that drives critical inquiry.

Bonaventure's starting point in *The Soul's Journey into God*, which many of my readers and I share, consists of the beliefs of the basic Christianity which are taught by Scripture and developed by tradition so that they can be embraced by individuals down through the ages. These beliefs include that there is a God who created the universe from nothing; that He is powerful, wise, and good; that He is a Trinity of three persons sharing a single divine essence; that He became human in the person of Jesus Christ, the God-man, who died to redeem human beings from sin. Bonaventure's starting point also includes the belief that St. Francis was blessed with a mystical vision of Christ in the form of a six-winged Seraph and received the stigmata as signs of divine favor; even if they are not required to share these particular beliefs as a matter of faith, Catholics and many other Christians do allow that such visions and physical occurrences are at least possible.

When we approach these beliefs in the spirit of critical inquiry guided by the desire to find the truth, we may discover that for some of them there are prima facie good reasons available to any rational investigator, whether or not he/she shares our faith. For other beliefs of basic Christianity, we may discover that there are no universally available, prima facie good reasons to hold them, but also no such reasons not to hold them either. Our confessing these beliefs as Christians, rather than suspending them as agnostics, may be justified if we can explain why there is some universally available, prima facie good reason for there being no universally available, prima facie good reasons for or against them; even so, we may have some other kind of reason for our holding these beliefs. We shall return to such cases in more depth in chapter 5, where we will examine stage four of the spiritual journey Bonaventure describes. Antecedent to our inquiry, there is no way of predicting on which side of the foregoing line the various beliefs of Christian orthodoxy will fall.

As Christians, we firmly believe that what we believe on faith will not turn out to be positively irrational. Other readers do not share this conviction, and even if we make a strong case for it they may very well have lingering doubts. We should respect their scruples no less than we would wish them to respect ours. Neither Bonaventure's treatise nor the way into Scholasticism we shall take from it is an excuse to proselytize, hector, or berate anyone. Just as the desire to find and understand the truth ought to be tempered by humility, so the desire to teach and expound truth ought to be tempered by an attitude of respect and charity towards those with whom we vehemently disagree even if our attitude may not always be reciprocated. We aim to conduct our enterprise in these pages in a spirit of peaceful intensity. Bonaventure speaks of "the peace proclaimed and given by our Lord Jesus

Christ and preached again and again by a father Francis."[5] He was "seeking this peace with panting spirit," and so he withdrew to Mount La Verna, "seeking a place of quiet and desiring to find there peace of spirit."[6] Let us reflect a bit on this *spirit of peace* and how we might cultivate it in the speculations upon which we are about to embark.

Much philosophy and theology practiced in academic circles today involves rough-and-tumble debate. Hardly an artifact of the modern era, this kind of disputation can be traced back to the medieval schools in the thirteenth and fourteenth centuries. Debate is a natural byproduct of the need for the propositions and arguments a thinker advances to be evaluated by the community of scholars. I do not wish to disparage intellectual dialogue or to dismiss the need for critical assessment by one's peers. However, all too often in the current climate, rough-and-tumble debate generates more heat than light, more acrimony than resolution, more pettiness than profundity, and more egotism than truth. Hence, following the example of St. Bonaventure, in this study we shall conduct speculative inquiry in a quieter, more meditative spirit that is closer to an intellectual retreat than to a scholarly disputation. The retreat begins with my expounding Bonaventure's text and addressing some issues it raises. Hopefully, the retreat will then expand beyond our study in these pages to encompass my readers in dialogue and even disagreement that nevertheless remains faithful to the contemplative mood of the retreat.

Finally, in approaching *The Soul's Journey into God* or any other piece of philosophical theology, including this

5. Ibid., 53.
6. Ibid., 54.

commentary, one would do well to follow Bonaventure's advice: "you should not run rapidly over the development of these considerations, but should mull them over slowly with the greatest care."[7] The linear presentation of philosophical theology in the form of premises, conclusions, sections, stages, chapters, and so forth belies the typically circuitous route of speculative inquiry. Perhaps the best approach combines linearity with a kind of relaxed engagement. I suggest reading Bonaventure's treatise all the way through at least once or twice to get a sense of the whole. Then, returning to the beginning, re-read each chapter of the treatise in conjunction with the corresponding chapter of my commentary. It is important to follow the order of *The Soul's Journey*, since later deliberations often build upon earlier ones. At each stage, feel free to set aside both treatise and commentary in order to absorb the ideas being presented. Take a walk, listen to some music, or enjoy a meal. Then, with renewed purpose, return to the relevant stage and pick up where you left off. You may be surprised to find that in the interim you have made considerable progress in your own thinking.

DISCUSSION QUESTION

Can Pascal's Revenge be avoided by suspending not only our belief that there is an independently existing world but also whether or not certain things like an evil deceiver or a wrathful God are even possible? Or when we suspend belief in something, does that still leave it open as a possibility? Is there any such thing as a neutral starting point in philosophy?

7. Ibid., 57.

Through Things to God

Bonaventure opens his account of the soul's journey with an admonition for anyone aspiring to attain mystical union with God as the highest good: "But we cannot rise above ourselves unless a higher power lifts us up. No matter how much our interior progress is ordered, nothing will come of it unless accompanied by divine aid."[1] After praying for divine guidance, Bonaventure takes his cue from St. Francis's vision of the six-winged Seraph and in the course of his treatise sketches six stages of illumination, culminating in ecstatic contemplation of God. The Seraphic Doctor distinguishes three perceptual or cognitive orientations (*aspectus principales*) of the human mind which recur throughout his account: turning outward toward external material objects, turning inward toward itself, or turning toward that which is "above" both external material objects and the human mind because not only is it

1. Bonaventure, *Soul's Journey into God*, 59.

external, and hence accessible to different minds, but it is also immaterial, and thus not limited by space and time.[2]

Furthermore, Bonaventure continues, with each of these orientations we can see God in one of two ways. We can see Him "through a mirror" when we recognize an external material object we perceive, a mental power we possess, or some concept and or principle we grasp as a sign, trace, or "vestige" (*vestigio*) indicating the existence of a transcendent God. Or we can see Him "in a mirror" by recognizing a certain creature as an image (*imago*) or a likeness (*similitudo*) of God. The result is a total of six stages of illumination, two corresponding to each mental orientation. Bonaventure allows for flexibility in the spiritual journey, advising that "we can consider each way independently or as joined to another."[3] Presumably, then, a seeker might immediately turn inward to consider his/her own mental powers as images of God. Yet since turning toward external material objects is a natural starting point, Bonaventure begins his description of the ascent at the bottom of "Jacob's ladder" by "presenting to ourselves the whole material world as a mirror through which we may pass over to God, the supreme Craftsman."[4]

For the moment, let us postpone examination of the distinction between seeing God "through a mirror" and seeing God "in a mirror," as well as the terms "vestige," "image," and "likeness." There is a more fundamental question whether the

2. See ibid., 61. An example of what Bonaventure has in mind by this third cognitive orientation is the commutativity of addition, which isn't merely a subjective idea in one person's mind but a law not limited to any particular place and time because it can be understood by mathematicians throughout history.

3. Ibid., 61.

4. Ibid., 63.

spiritual journey Bonaventure outlines has any philosophical significance at all. At first glance, his assertion that nothing will come of the spiritual journey unless the seeker receives divine aid sought through prayer seems to imply a negative answer. If the sincere seeker prays for divine guidance, then she already believes that there is a God who possesses all the attributes Bonaventure tries to derive in the course of his treatise. Such a seeker is in need, not of philosophical arguments, but of a method enabling her to attain mystical union with the God in whom she has faith. On the other hand, it seems that someone who is sincerely skeptical about the existence of such a God won't be helped by the kind of spiritual journey Bonaventure describes, since the journey requires the skeptic to pray to the very being whose existence he doubts!

Two pieces of textual evidence point a way out of this apparent impasse. First, Bonaventure elaborates on the place of prayer in the spiritual journey:

> Since grace is the foundation of the rectitude of the will and of the penetrating light of reason, we must first pray, then live holy lives and thirdly concentrate our attention upon the reflections of truth. By concentrating there, we must ascend step by step until we reach the height of the mountain *where the God of gods is seen in Zion* [Vulgate Ps. 83:8].[5]

The operative phrase in this passage is "step by step." Bonaventure doesn't say that *each* step of the spiritual journey requires prayer, which in turn presupposes faith in God. A more careful reading of the passage is that faith and prayer are necessary to complete *all* the steps leading to the sum-

5. Ibid., 63.

mit of mystical ecstasy. Specifically, the reflections presented at some of steps of the journey might have probative force even for someone who does not already believe in the God of Christian orthodoxy.

The second piece of textual evidence indicates that Bonaventure intends the first stage of the journey, where God is contemplated in His vestiges in the universe, indeed to provide rational warrant for believing that there is a God who is the First Principle of all creatures. At the conclusion of his first chapter Bonaventure writes,

> Whoever, therefore, is not enlightened by such splendor of created things is blind; whoever does not praise God because of all these effects is dumb; *whoever does not discover the First Principle from such clear signs* [emphasis added] is a fool. Therefore, open your eyes, alert the ears of your spirit, open your lips and *apply your heart* so that in all creatures you may see, hear, praise, love, worship, glorify and honor your God lest the whole world rise against you.[6]

Bonaventure doesn't say "whoever is a Christian" but simply "whoever" does not discover the First Principle from such clear signs is a fool—including whoever is not already a Christian. This strong statement makes no sense unless Bonaventure takes himself to have adduced reasons that should convince even a skeptic that God as First Principle exists. What, then, are these reasons?

Bonaventure argues that God's power, wisdom, and goodness are reflected in the properties of external mate-

6. Ibid., 67–68.

rial objects. These objects have weight, which is their power of attraction toward the center of the earth. Moreover, they don't coalesce into a mass of gunk but can be numbered and counted, thus manifesting a kind of natural intelligibility or wisdom. And the boundaries of a material object are beneficial because by limiting a particular object (e.g., this tree) to here rather than allowing it to expand to over there (e.g., where there's fire) they preserve the object from immediate destruction, thus manifesting natural goodness. Concerning the entire material universe itself, Bonaventure observes that it originates, or at least that later states of the universe originate from earlier states. These acts of origination involve causality, which indicates power. Additionally, the processes in the material universe aren't chaotic but occur in accordance with natural laws which are another mark of natural wisdom; and the universe (or at least many of the entities in it, such as rain watering the grass so it will grow) tends toward beneficial ends, another indication of natural goodness. Finally, the ordering of the material universe into different kinds of things—minerals, vegetables, animals, and the various species within these genera—also signifies power, wisdom, and goodness, since each kind exercises its own characteristic power (e.g., birds fly), possesses its own complex nature (e.g., diamonds exhibit an intricate crystalline structure), and tends to its own proper end (e.g., an oak seed matures into an oak tree). Bonaventure concludes: "From these visible things, therefore, one rises to consider the power, wisdom, and goodness of God as existing, living, intelligent, purely spiritual, incorruptible, and unchangeable."[7]

7. Ibid., 64–65.

If this is Bonaventure's argument for inferring the existence of a powerful, wise, and good God from the properties of the material universe, then it is unconvincing. Granting that there are numerous instances of natural power, intelligibility, and beneficial functioning like those Bonaventure adumbrates, so far they provide no logical reason for deducing the existence of a transcendent being or "First Principle" who is powerful, wise, and good and manifests these attributes by creating the material universe. Perhaps there is nothing more than the natural power, "wisdom"/intelligibility, and "goodness"/beneficial functioning we find distributed throughout the material universe itself.

Does the presence of power, intelligibility, and beneficial functioning in the universe provide, if not a purely deductive reason, then at least strong inductive evidence for the existence of a transcendent First Principle who is powerful, wise, and good? Bonaventure does speak of passing over from the material world to "God, the supreme Craftsman." Just as encountering a tremendously tall and massive, technically sophisticated edifice that ensures temperate weather for the creatures in its vicinity would constitute compelling evidence, though not deductive proof, that the edifice was the product of a being sufficiently powerful, wise, and benevolent to create the edifice, so the same might be true of the entire material universe itself.[8] The main difficulty with this argument is that it overlooks the numerous instances of natural weakness,

8. This kind of argument would place Bonaventure in the company of the eighteenth-century English theologian William Paley, who compares the complexity of the universe to the complexity of a watch: just as the latter complexity provides sufficient inductive evidence for an intelligent watchmaker, Paley argues, so the former complexity provides sufficient inductive evidence for an intelligent designer of the universe.

unintelligibility, and harmful functioning throughout the material universe. Defective creatures fail to survive, random lightning strikes coupled with severe earthquakes in the same region don't really make sense, and deadly pathogens destroy millions of innocent lives. Once this countervailing evidence in the material universe is factored into the equation, at best the empirical case for a powerful, wise, and good Craftsman is inconclusive.

However, Bonaventure continues:

> This reflection can be extended according to the sevenfold properties of creatures—which is a sevenfold testimony to the divine power, wisdom, and goodness—if we consider the origin, magnitude, multitude, beauty, fullness, activity, and order of things.[9]

"The sevenfold properties of creatures" Bonaventure mentions are the most general characteristics exhibited by things in the material universe. The characteristics in question are trans-categorical because they are exhibited by entirely different kinds of things; for example, rocks and birds both have origins. In each case, Bonaventure observes that exhibiting the relevant trans-categorical characteristic is also a way of exhibiting the triple property of power, wisdom, and goodness. Let us look more closely at each trans-categorical characteristic, using contemporary examples to underscore the continuing relevance of Bonaventure's observations.[10]

Origin: Material things originate from other material things through the exercise of causal power. Geological up-

9. Ibid., 65.
10. See ibid., 65–67.

heavals cause the formation of mountains and seas; the sun causes seeds to sprout; by reproducing, plants, animals, and human beings cause other beings of their respective kinds to exist. Obviously, whatever exercises causal power through origination exhibits power. Moreover, since origination of material things through causal power conforms to intelligible laws of nature, whatever exercises this causal power also exhibits wisdom in the sense of basic intelligibility.[11] Finally, the origination of material things through intelligible causal power can be ranked or evaluated in terms of goodness: of two seismic events, the one that gives rise to a mountain range is better qua seismic event than the one that gives rise to only a single hill; of two fig trees, the one that regularly produces more figs is the better fig tree; of two wolves, the one procreating more and stronger cubs is the better wolf. Thus material things which exercise intelligible causal power through origination also exhibit goodness to varying degrees. Therefore, these things exhibit the triple property of power, wisdom, and goodness.

Magnitude: Bonaventure next turns his attention to the trans-categorical characteristic of material things which remain stable while extending over a definite and often considerable area. A granite mountain of great length, width, and depth that maintains its structural integrity for eons, intense sunlight that illuminates numerous terrestrial objects, and a fire that consumes a redwood forest all exhibit tremendous power. These phenomena also possess intrinsic, highly complex structures—the layers of geologic strata constituting the

11. Why Bonaventure thinks that this basic intelligibility indicates something like human wisdom will become apparent in the course of his argument.

mountain, the particle-wave duality of light, and the chemical reactions in the fire releasing light and heat and resulting in the exothermic oxidation of combustible substances—that make sense, and hence exhibit wisdom as intelligibility. Finally, no less than causal processes, things of great magnitude can be ranked or evaluated in terms of goodness: the better mountain is the one that endures the elements longer; the better light the one that illuminates more objects; the better fire the one that releases more thermodynamic energy. Consequently, things exhibiting the property of magnitude also exhibit the triple property of power, intelligibility or wisdom, and goodness.

Multitude: Not only individual things in the material universe but groups of them exhibit power, wisdom, and goodness. Take a school of whales. As a collective body, it exercises causal power (e.g., by swimming through the ocean), manifests highly intelligible patterns (e.g., sophisticated migration and communication behaviors we are only beginning to fathom), and pursues objectives which are good for the individual whales as well as for the entire school (e.g., feeding, fighting off attackers, producing more offspring). Other multitudes in the material universe exhibit the same triple property of power, wisdom, and goodness to lesser or greater degrees.

Beauty: Different kinds of things—minerals, flowers, predators like tigers or leopards or jaguars, stars, and human bodies—possess pleasing aesthetic qualities that elicit powerful responses in us. Thus beautiful things exhibit power. Part of what makes a thing beautiful is the (sometimes unexpected) harmony and proportion of its features or parts. Since intelligibility includes aesthetic harmony and proportion, beautiful things exhibit intelligibility. Clearly, the more a beautiful thing, such as a Greek Corinthian column or an Elizabethan sonnet, realizes the harmony and proportion appropriate to that sort of work, the better it is in strictly artistic terms. Accordingly, beautiful things also exhibit goodness, and hence exhibit the triple property of power, wisdom, and goodness.

Fullness: Bonaventure speaks of "seminal reasons," a notion he inherits from St. Augustine. Without examining this notion in detail, we can indicate the trans-categorical characteristic of things in the material universe that Bonaventure is describing here. Some things are potentially other things; for example, an oak seedling is potentially an oak tree and a human embryo is potentially an adult human person. The unfolding of these potentialities through the natural process of growth exhibits the power of becoming. Furthermore, these potentialities exhibit natural intelligibility, since what explains why the seedling grows into an oak as opposed to an elm and why the embryo grows into a human person rather than a chimpanzee are the distinct structures intrinsic to each of these potentialities that to a certain extent can be identified and studied, as in the case of DNA. Finally, to the extent a natural potentiality develops in accordance with its intrinsic structure, it exhibits a degree of natural goodness. An oak seedling that naturally develops into a towering oak that lives for over a hundred years is better than one that generates a sickly shoot lasting only a week. Therefore, things which exhibit fullness or potentiality also exhibit the triple property of power, wisdom, and goodness.

Activity: So far, Bonaventure has concentrated primarily on natural power, goodness, and intelligibility or wisdom.

He now calls our attention to the diverse levels of activity throughout the material universe. Some of this activity is purely natural, in that it is neither the result of human artifice nor susceptible to moral evaluation. The activity of an ant colony isn't something we orchestrate, and the ants aren't morally bad for stealing crumbs from a picnic. Other activities are a matter of human artifice even if they needn't be morally good or morally bad. A human composer, a human conductor, and human performers devise, direct, and execute the activity of playing a symphony that is then judged good or bad in artistic rather than moral terms. Yet other activities we opt to undertake are also subject to moral evaluation. We raise children, broker business agreements, and form political communities; how we engage in these activities can be judged morally bad (e.g., abusing, swindling, tyrannizing) or morally good (nurturing, honoring, protecting, and promoting). Many examples of activity at each of these three levels exhibit causal power because they accomplish results; intelligibility because they follow laws, rules, or principles either instinctively, as with the ants, or deliberately, as with us; and good because they are naturally beneficial, aesthetically pleasing, or morally right. Therefore, the manifold activity of things all around us exhibits the triple property of power, wisdom, and goodness. We begin to see that, for Bonaventure, the fundamental power, intelligibility, and goodness manifested in the material universe is not limited to any one kind of power, intelligibility, and goodness found in the material universe.

Order: Material entities and processes can be numbered and counted. They have spatial dimensions and temporal durations which can be measured. Many material things also stand in definite relations of causal dependence; for example, photosynthesis causally depends on solar irradiation but not vice versa. Other things are higher or lower in terms of their relative complexity—human beings are higher life forms than amoebas—and we have already noted the purely natural, artificial, and moral levels of both individual and collective activity. All these forms of order and hierarchy throughout the material universe contribute to its intelligibility. In addition, order is often a way of exhibiting power. An example from nature is the functioning of an ecosystem containing numerous levels of creatures and environmental resources as in a food chain. An example from the artistic sphere is the order and discipline among the members of an orchestra that is required to perform a Beethoven symphony. An example from society is the institutional hierarchy of a volunteer organization like a church that enables the church to provide services and benefits effectively and efficiently to those in need. These cases also make clear that order is often a way of exhibiting natural goodness (survival and propagation of higher life forms), aesthetic goodness (a superb performance), and moral goodness (charity).

Having completed his description of how the transcategorical characteristics of material things exhibit the triple property of power, wisdom, and goodness, Bonaventure proclaims: "Whoever, therefore, is not enlightened by such splendor of created things is blind; whoever does not praise God because of all these effects is dumb; whoever does not discover the First Principle from such clear signs is a fool." We are now in a position, I believe, to see why his bold statement isn't simply a dogmatic declaration but instead the conclusion of a substantial metaphysical argument I will call Bonaventure's *proof by exclusion*.

The proof by exclusion runs as follows. There is a triple property of power, wisdom, and goodness. For, as Bonaventure's description shows, this triple property is exhibited by any particular thing or collection of things in the material universe exhibiting one of the seven trans-categorical characteristics of origin, magnitude, multitude, beauty, fullness, activity, or order. However, the triple property of power, wisdom, and goodness is not identical with any of these seven trans-categorical characteristics. For suppose it were. Then the triple property would reduce to one of the seven trans-categorical characteristics of material things—for example, it would reduce to magnitude. But then any particular material thing or collection of material things could only exhibit power, wisdom, and goodness by exhibiting magnitude. Such a consequence is absurd. The power, wisdom (intelligibility), and goodness exhibited by the potentiality of a miniscule human embryo has nothing to with magnitude! Or if the triple property reduced to the trans-categorical characteristic of activity, then the only way for a mountain to exhibit power, wisdom, and goodness would for the mountain to be active—which is ridiculous, given that the mountain is inert. A multitude of ugly cockroaches cannot exhibit power, wisdom, and goodness by being beautiful, nor can an awesome firestorm that destroys an entire forest exhibit power wisdom and goodness by originating anything. So, reducing this triple property to any one of the seven trans-categorical characteristics would entail that many material things which obviously exhibit power, wisdom, and goodness cannot exhibit it. Hence the triple property of power, wisdom, and goodness exhibited by things in the material universe is not identical with any trans-categorical characteristic of material things. Nonetheless, it is a real property. To be a real property distinct from any trans-categorical characteristic of things in the material universe, it must also be an attribute of something not in the material universe. This transcendent entity possessing the attribute of power, wisdom, and goodness—a property that is also exhibited in varying degrees by things in the material universe—is the First Principle, or God. Therefore, the First Principle exists.

Let us draw out the proof by exclusion a bit by considering four possible objections to it. First, the argument assumes that Bonaventure's list of the trans-categorical characteristics is complete. What if material things also exhibit power, wisdom, and goodness by exhibiting some other trans-categorical characteristic, perhaps one overlooked by Bonaventure or hitherto undiscovered by us? It is difficult to see how the existence of an unlisted characteristic C would affect the basic thrust of Bonaventure's argument. For either C is simply identical with the triple property of power, wisdom, and goodness exhibited by material things insofar as they exhibit the other trans-categorical characteristics besides C, or C is not identical with the triple property. If C is identical with the triple property, then as before we reach the absurd result that the only way for a material thing or group of material things lacking C to exhibit power, wisdom, and goodness is for it to exhibit C, which is impossible. On the other hand, if C is *not* identical with the triple property of power, wisdom, and goodness, then by Bonaventure's argument a material thing or group of material things possessing C exhibits power, wisdom, and goodness not by exhibiting some other trans-categorical characteristic besides C, which again is absurd, but by exhibiting to some degree the power, wisdom, and goodness of the transcendent First Principle.

Another possible objection has its roots in the ontology of Plato. Plato maintains that the things of this world have properties which themselves are not of this world. These properties are Forms which primarily exist not in our minds or in space and time but in an abstract "third realm" beyond human minds, space, and time. According to Plato, although material things participate in these transcendent Forms, it isn't necessarily the case that in order for a Form to be a real property there must also be some non-material thing that participates in the Form. A Platonist might grant that there is a triple property of power, wisdom, and goodness distinct from any trans-categorical characteristic of material things yet deny that the transcendent triple property is an attribute of something not in the material universe. For the transcendent triple property could be a Platonic Form.

A problem with this objection is that it leaves us without any clear way of explaining *why* the triple property of power, wisdom, and goodness isn't one of the seven trans-categorical characteristics of material things. On the Platonic view, these characteristics are all Forms, too. The triple property can't be one of these characteristics since, as we have seen, supposing the contrary leads to absurdity. But what is the *real basis* in virtue of which it can't be one of them? Intuitively, if two Forms are really distinct then there should be some fact of the matter that accounts for why they are distinct. Yet in the case of the triple property and the trans-categorical characteristics, the Platonic objection offers no indication of what constitutes the real distinction between them. By contrast, Bonaventure's position does: Unlike each of the seven trans-categorical characteristics, which can only be exhibited by things in the material universe, the triple property of power, wisdom, and goodness is not only exhibited to some degree by these things but also by something not in the material universe.[12]

A third possible objection is that the power, wisdom, and goodness making up the transcendent triple property need not be the kind of "power," "wisdom," and "goodness" exhibited by someone endowed with agency, wisdom, and moral goodness. Why aren't "power," "wisdom," and "goodness" at the transcendent level wholly non-personal, like the power of a thunderstorm, the intelligibility of a chemical reaction, and the goodness of a ripe apple, respectively?

In reply, Bonaventure might point out that the triple property of power, wisdom, and goodness is a single, unified property. As such, it is not only exhibited by thunderstorms, chemical reactions, and ripe apples but also by human legislators forming a community guided by laws and principles in a manner resulting in justice. Thus the transcendent triple property of power, wisdom, and goodness must encompass the power of persons, which is agency; the intelligibility involved in persons' prudent decisions, which is wisdom; and virtue of persons, which is moral goodness. Since the triple property is also an attribute of something not in the material

12. In the next chapter we shall encounter another reason Bonaventure might give for denying that distinct Forms co-exist in a non-spatiotemporal "third realm." It should also be noted that since the triple property of power, wisdom, and goodness applies to beings from different genera (for example, mountains in the genus *mineral* and whales in the genus *animal*), the triple property itself is not a genus of things in the material universe that exists in them through specific differences (as the genus *animal* exists in human beings through the specific difference *rational*).

universe, this something must exhibit power, wisdom, and goodness in a way that includes but isn't limited to human power, wisdom, and moral goodness. For if this something exhibits power, wisdom, and goodness in a way that doesn't include the human manifestations of these properties, then it is indistinguishable from some non-human, impersonal thing in the material universe. And if this something exhibits power, wisdom, and goodness in a way that is limited to human power, wisdom, and moral goodness then it is indistinguishable from a human thing in the material universe.[13] Both alternatives are excluded by the fact that the something in question is not in the material universe. So this non-material something exhibits agency, wisdom, and moral goodness greater than human agency, wisdom, and moral goodness. Therefore, the something in question is *someone*: namely, the First Principle, who possesses agency, wisdom, and moral goodness to an even greater degree than we do.

Finally, it might be objected that the presence of weakness, foolishness, and badness in the material universe renders Bonaventure's proof by exclusion just as inconclusive as the arguments we considered earlier in this chapter. However, the existence of material things exhibiting weakness, foolishness, and badness doesn't negate the existence of other material things exhibiting power, wisdom, and goodness by exhibiting one of the seven trans-categorical properties Bonaventure describes. The logical inference to a transcendent, triple property of power, wisdom, and goodness that is

13. It is possible that humans are things in the material universe without being entirely material things. In particular, a human might be a unity of a material thing—its body—and a non-material thing—its soul.

also an attribute of something not in the material universe remains intact. Once the existence of a First Principle who possesses agency, wisdom, and moral goodness greater than the merely human versions of these attributes is taken seriously, we must also take seriously the idea of Providence: that the First Principle may turn whatever weakness, foolishness, and badness exists in the material universe ultimately to a positive outcome in which these deficiencies are overcome.

A fair verdict is that Bonaventure's account of the first stage of the soul's journey yields a prima facie plausible proof for the existence of God as a transcendent First Principle. The proof relies upon definite metaphysical assumptions: that material things have real properties; that these properties themselves are real things rather than mere mental concepts; that if real properties are distinct then there must be a real basis for the distinction between them; that the power, wisdom, and goodness exhibited by material things and by God is a unitary property; and that different things can exhibit this same property to different degrees. Admittedly, it is possible to resist Bonaventure's proof by rejecting any one or even all of these assumptions. In other words, Scholastic philosophical theology of the kind exemplified by Bonaventure's proof by exclusion doesn't nail everything down forever but invites ongoing discussion. So far, though, Bonaventure's project has been successful.

We conclude this chapter by returning to Bonaventure's use of the term "vestige." Vestiges are things which indicate God's existence "through a mirror." I have postponed discussion of the term, preferring to lay out Bonaventure's proof by exclusion first because I believe that this kind of argument provides the proper context for understanding what

Bonaventure means by "vestige." Something in the universe is a vestige if it exhibits a property the full analysis (*plene resolvens*) of which leads to an attribute possessed by God. We shall encounter a similar proof by exclusion in Bonaventure's account of stage three of the soul's journey, where he claims that our mental powers as inner things are also vestiges of God. There, we shall consider an anti-metaphysical objection to this kind of metaphysical argument, as well as how a metaphysician like Bonaventure might address it.

Discussion Questions

(1) Does Bonaventure's metaphysical argument rule out the possibility of more than one First Principle existing, or the possibility of a First Principle previously existing but no longer existing?

(2) What does it mean to say that the First Principle possesses agency, wisdom, and moral goodness to an even greater degree than we human beings do?

  (a) Does it mean that the First Principle possesses these properties in exactly the sense we do yet without any limitation, comparable to how a finite number and an infinite number are nonetheless both numbers?

  (b) Or does it mean that the agency, wisdom, and moral goodness of the First Principle both resembles and differs from our agency, wisdom, and moral goodness, comparable to how our intelligence both resembles and differs from a dog's intelligence?

(3) How does the relation between the First Principle and the triple property of power, wisdom, and goodness differ from the relation between material things and this property? Can material things exhibit the triple property only by possessing some characteristic (e.g., magnitude) that is distinct from the property, whereas the First Principle exhibits the triple property without having to possess a distinct characteristic (so that the First Principle *exemplifies* power, wisdom, and goodness)?

THREE

Our Senses and the Divine Mosaic

Recall that Bonaventure distinguishes between our seeing God "through a mirror," when we recognize things in the universe as vestiges which indicate His existence, and our seeing God "in a mirror," when we recognize things in the universe as images or likenesses of Him. In the previous chapter we examined Bonaventure's reasons for thinking that external material things are vestiges of God. In this chapter we shall consider Bonaventure's account of how some internal things, particularly our sensory activities, are images of God.

According to Bonaventure, "this type of consideration is higher than the previous one"[1] because

> For these creatures [of the sense world] are shadows, echoes, and pictures of that first, most powerful, most wise and most perfect Principle, of that eternal Source, Light and Fullness, of that efficient,

1. Bonaventure, *Soul's Journey into God*, 69.

> exemplary and ordering Art. They are vestiges,
> representations, spectacles proposed to us and
> signs divinely given so that we can see God.[2]

Bonaventure's use of the term "vestiges" in this passage can make it hard to see why the second stage of the ascent is higher than the first, since the first stage concerns vestiges as well. However, Bonaventure also employs the terms "pictures" and "representations," providing a clue about the difference between things which are merely vestiges and things which are images or likenesses. A picture or representation literally depicts what it pictures or represents. So whatever "these creatures of the sense world" are exactly, as images they must somehow literally depict God. By contrast, a mere vestige, such as a mountain in the Rockies, doesn't literally picture, represent, or depict God—though, through exhibiting immensity, it does exhibit His power, wisdom, and goodness.[3] The question of why Bonaventure thinks that our sensory activities literally depict God will occupy us shortly.

As with the previous stage, Bonaventure infers a particularly strong conclusion from his reflections on sensory things:

> From all [of] this, one can gather that *from the creation of the world the invisible attributes of God are clearly seen, being understood through the things that are made* [Rom. 1:2]. And so those who do not

2. Ibid., 76.

3. Since at least some of the seven trans-categorical characterizations apply to any material thing in the universe, we might say that images are those vestiges which, in addition to being vestiges, also depict God. The difference between an "image" and a "likeness" will be discussed in chapter 5.

wish to heed these things, and to know, bless, and
love God in all of them *are without excuse*; for they
are unwilling to be transported *out of darkness into
the marvelous light* of God.[4]

Hence Bonaventure thinks that it is possible even for a skeptic to see and know God in the sensory things which are images of divinity. One need not already believe in the God of
Christian orthodoxy for the reflections at this stage to have
probative force.

To understand the basic idea behind his reflections, it
helps to appreciate how Bonaventure weaves together aspects
of both Aristotelian epistemology and Platonic metaphysics.
This eclectic strategy is motivated by Bonaventure's desire
to make the strongest possible case for his position based
on the best philosophical resources available to him and his
audience. His approach raises two questions we shall want to
track. The first is whether Bonaventure's mélange of Platonic
and Aristotelian elements is a misguided attempt to mix oil
and water, or rather a convincing example of the whole being greater than the sum of its parts. The second question is
whether the philosophical resources Bonaventure relies upon
in making his case can be rendered plausible, or even accessible, to a contemporary audience. With these two questions
in mind, we now turn to the details of Bonaventure's case.

Bonaventure writes, "It should be noted that this world,
which is called the macrocosm, enters our soul, which is
called the smaller world, through the doors of the five senses
as we perceive, enjoy, and judge sensible things."[5] By "the

4. Ibid., 77.
5. Ibid., 69.

macrocosm," he means the entire world of stars, trees, rocks, liquids, noises, odors, and everything else in the external world available to us through sensation. Our sensory experiences of these external things are internal and proper to our respective minds: I can't share your taste of the piece of pineapple you just popped into your mouth. On the basis of our diverse sensory experiences, however, each of us builds up a mental picture of external reality that is more or less accurate. (Otherwise none of us would survive for very long!) This mental picture of external reality is what Bonaventure means by "the smaller world," or microcosm, whereby the macrocosm enters the soul through sensory experience. He discerns perception or apprehension, pleasure, and judgment as three parts of the human sensory process.

When you see an elm tree or hear running water or taste a piece of pineapple or smell smoke or touch a rock, the tree, water, pineapple, smoke, and rock do not literally enter your mind. Instead,

> These exterior sense objects are the first which enter into the soul through the gate of the five senses. They enter, I say, not through their substance, but through their likenesses, which are first produced in the medium; and from the medium they enter into the organ and from the exterior organ into the interior organ and from this into the apprehensive faculty.[6]

The notion of sensory likenesses (*similitudines*) is an idea Bonaventure takes from Aristotelian epistemology as com-

---

6. Ibid., 71.

monly interpreted by medieval thinkers.[7] On this interpretation, any external thing such as an elm tree has a real nature, or substantial form, that it shares with every other thing of the same kind. When you see an elm, the form existing substantially in the tree is transmitted through the medium of light to your eye, where this exact same form then exists non-substantially—i.e., independently of the material conditions determining how it exists in the elm, although the form also continues to exist substantially in the elm as well. The form existing non-substantially in your eye provides visual information about that particular elm so that you apprehend it; as the same form comes to exist non-substantially in your other senses your mind apprehends more of the elm's sensible properties. In a similar way, the substantial forms of other elms can come to exist non-substantially in your senses. Higher cognitive processes enable you to analyze this additional information in order to apprehend what all elms have in common: asymmetrical bases, curving branches, serrated and deciduous leaves, etc. Without deciding whether the medieval interpretation of Aristotle is correct, we can at least admit that the exact same information inherent in external objects is transmittable through a medium to our sensory experiences. For example, based on her visual experience of the elm in good light an observer can accurately estimate its height at twenty-five feet and the number of its branches at sixteen. The measurements retrieved from her experience are

7. Aristotle presents his theory of perception in *De anima*. For Bonaventure's appropriation of this theory, see Book 2 of *Commentaries on the Four Books of Sentences of Peter Lombard*—especially point 2 on 570, where Bonaventure speaks of "the corporal organ, in which phantasms [forms abstracted from their material conditions in external things] are received."

identical with the measurements actually embodied in the tree.

Under the right conditions, when the form of an external object is transmitted through a medium and then comes to exist non-substantially in your senses, your mind takes pleasure in the object it perceives. Visual information you receive about the elm may include the graceful symmetry of its trunk and branches. Auditory and tactile information about the running water may include its soft gurgling and coolness. In each case, the sensory information produces in you an agreeable effect. Such agreeableness requires that "the acting power does not proportionally exceed the recipient"[8]; for example, perceiving the elm in glaring light or perceiving the deafening roar of icy floodwaters is certainly not pleasant. Since "the senses are pained by extremes,"[9] instances where the senses exceed the acting power, such as squinting at the elm in weak light or straining to hear a low voice, aren't agreeable either. Yet as long as information about the object is transmitted to the senses without exceeding or being exceeded by them, any pain or discord in the act of perception is avoided. The more harmony is present in the received sensory information about the object, and hence in the object itself, the more pleasure, even delight, the mind takes in perceiving that object. Sometimes, as in touching and tasting the water in consuming it, additional pleasure is provided through nourishment of the recipient.

The sensory information we receive about external objects we apprehend and enjoy also forms the basis for our judgment about these objects. By "judgment," Bonaventure

8. Bonaventure, *Soul's Journey into God*, 71.
9. Ibid.

means not only perceptual judgments of fact—e.g., the water is cold—but evaluations. When you sample a glass of fine Bordeaux, in addition to apprehending and enjoying the wine's clear ruby color you may discern a perfect balance on the tongue between the tannins, acid, sweetness, and alcohol. Or when you see the elm you appreciate its symmetry. The wine's balance and the elm's symmetry are ultimately proportions of harmony abstracting from the spatial and temporal relations of size, duration, and motion. Whether the amount of wine is only a thimbleful or an entire vat, whether the wine lasts in its premium state for only a few seconds or for a million years, whether the wine is moving or at rest, the perfect balance of its components remains constant. Similarly, the symmetry abstracted from the elm is a numeric relationship not dependent on how large the elm is, how long it endures, whether or not the wind is stirring its branches, or even whether the elm exists at all.[10]

It is precisely here that Bonaventure gives his Aristotelian epistemology of sensory experience a Platonic metaphysical twist: "It [harmony] abstracts, therefore, from place, time, and motion, and consequently is unchangeable, unlimited, endless, and completely spiritual."[11] The Platonic Forms men-

10. Bonaventure takes proportions of harmony to include musical harmonies and rhythms, rhythms in dance and other forms of gestures, and every sort of ratio. He follows St. Augustine in subsuming these proportions, along with quantities, magnitudes, mathematical series and orderings, under the general concept of number; see ibid., 74–75. Bonaventure may be partly motivated by the fact that while shape, size, and duration are obviously spatiotemporal quantities of external objects, these quantities can ultimately be described in numeric terms which are independent of spatiotemporal reality.

11. Ibid., 72.

tioned in the previous chapter are examples *par excellence* of entities which are unchangeable, are unlimited by spatial boundaries, are without beginning and without end in terms of temporal duration, and are non-material or spiritual. Bonaventure is saying that the forms existing both substantially in external objects and non-substantially in our senses resemble Forms in that they exist beyond all space and time. We might wonder why something that exists both substantially in an object and non-substantially in us exists beyond all space and time, since obviously both we and the object are in space and time. Or is the foregoing observation simply another way of making Bonaventure's point? If the existence of one and the same form isn't restricted to the spatiotemporal location of the object I perceive or to my spatiotemporal location when I am perceiving it, then the form's fundamental existence doesn't appear to depend on any particular spatiotemporal location, making it a non-spatiotemporal entity to which different temporal things, such as minds and the objects they perceive, stand in distinct relations. Later in the chapter we shall return to this important issue, as well as to the question of why Bonaventure thinks these non-spatiotemporal entities differ from Platonic Forms.

Having reviewed the three aspects of the sensory process by which we build up an accurate mental picture of external reality, Bonaventure claims that "All these are vestiges in which we can see our God."[12] When we apprehend an external object, the object generates a form in our senses that is not only a perfect likeness of the form in the object but also one in being with it. Yet there remains some ontologi-

12. Ibid.

cal distinction here, since the same form that exists substantially in the object exists non-substantially in our senses. To Bonaventure, this metaphysical situation reflects on a smaller scale the eternal generation by the Father of the Son, who is not only a perfect likeness of the Father but also one in being with Him while remaining an ontologically distinct person. In Bonaventure's view, the parallel is reinforced by the fact that just as uniting a form with the human senses leads us to apprehend the object itself, so uniting the Son with human flesh in the Incarnation leads us to the Father Himself "as to the fountain-source and object."[13]

Furthermore, judging or evaluating the sensory information we receive reveals proportions of harmony which, like Platonic Forms, are unlimited by space and endless in terms of time. Bonaventure argues that since whatever is "unlimited and endless" is eternal and "Everything that is eternal is either God or in God,"[14] it follows that these non-spatiotemporal entities are ideas eternally existing in the divine wisdom and also literally existing *in us* whenever we perceive external objects through our senses. Bonaventure calls the totality of these divine ideas, which encompasses all possible proportions of harmony, "the Eternal Art, by which, through which and according to which all beautiful things are formed."[15] He identifies the Eternal Art with the Son.[16]

13. Ibid., 72–73.

14. Ibid., 73.

15. Ibid., 74.

16. I have altered Bonaventure's order of exposition by presenting the image of God in sensory evaluation before the image of God in sensory delight, since Bonaventure's reasons for thinking that our sensory delight reflects God's delight in knowing His own being through the Son becomes somewhat clearer once the Son is identified with the Eternal Art.

These considerations lead Bonaventure to regard our delight in perceiving objects through sensory forms as a reflection of God's primordial delight in knowing His own being through "that first Species,"[17] the Son. The Son is a perfect likeness eternally generated by God. In eternally generating the Son God knows His own being, including His eternal generation of the Son in virtue of which God is the Father. The Son is one in being with God generating the Son, so that the Son neither exceeds nor is exceeded by the divine knower. Hence there is no pain or discord in God knowing His being through the Son. The Son is also the Eternal Art encompassing all possible proportions of harmony, so that these divine ideas equally pertain to God the Father with whom the Son is one in being. Hence in God knowing His own being through the Son there is also a maximum of harmony—"the union of the harmonious with the harmonious."[18] In other words, God supremely delights in knowing His own being this way, just as we delight in knowing the being of external objects through their harmonious forms which neither exceed nor are exceeded by our senses receiving them.

The last three paragraphs went by fast. Let us slow the pace by considering an objection to what has been said so far. Assume that Bonaventure's Aristotelian description of the human sensory process is accurate. Specifically, then, when I see the elm, the form of symmetry existing substantially in the tree is transmitted through the medium of light to my eye, where the same form then exists non-substantially. Thus the form isn't restricted to the spatiotemporal location of the elm, the spatiotemporal location of my eye, or any other spatio-

17. Ibid., 73.
18. Ibid.

temporal location since the form can be propagated through the medium in any direction. However, it doesn't automatically follow that the form of symmetry is entirely non-spatiotemporal. For it may still be true that the form has to exist in *some* spatiotemporal location or other, though not in any *particular* spatiotemporal location. A thought experiment clarifies this point. If there were no elm trees, no medium of light, and no human perceivers, it is hardly obvious that the form of symmetry I see in the elm would still somehow exist. *Where* would it exist? Not in any elms, for there are none. Nor would the form exist in the medium the way information about a long-ago extinguished star still does, since there is no medium. Not in human minds, for in the envisaged scenario there aren't any of those either. Without any spatiotemporal location where the form of symmetry exists, it is difficult to fathom how it would exist at all.

The same point applies to other harmonic proportions and numeric relationships. Three-sided objects and human thoughts of them may come and go, so that the form of being triangular doesn't depend on any one of these objects or thoughts. But if there were *no* three-sided objects or thoughts of them, then the form of being triangular wouldn't exist in any straightforward sense either. Without a clear reason for thinking that there are purely non-spatiotemporal forms, Bonaventure's argument that divine ideas exist in us whenever we perceive external objects can't get off the ground. For if there is nothing non-spatiotemporal in us whenever we perceive, then Bonaventure cannot argue from these non-spatiotemporal entities to their eternity and from their eternity to their divinity.

We saw that in his account of the first stage of the soul's journey Bonaventure gives a plausible proof by exclusion for God's existence as a transcendent First Principle possessing the triple property of power, wisdom, and goodness. Based on what he has already shown, can Bonaventure derive the existence of divine ideas as non-spatiotemporal entities eternally existing in God and also existing in us whenever we perceive external objects through our senses? If a First Principle exists then presumably its wisdom includes ideas of every actual and possible being. In particular, even before the creation of the world when there weren't any elms with symmetry or any triangles or any human minds yet, the First Principle had ideas of all these possible beings. Since the First Principle is transcendent, its wisdom and hence its ideas are beyond space and time.

The problem with this interpretation is that it gives us no reason to think that non-spatiotemporal aspects of divine wisdom corresponding to actual and possible beings ever literally exist *in us*. Bonaventure's present goal is to show how we can see God "in the mirror" of the human sensory process, not just "through the mirror" of His vestiges in the universe. At best, the argument of the previous paragraph only establishes that divine ideas exist beyond space and time, not that these same ideas exist in us whenever we perceive external objects. Bonaventure seems to be confronted with a dilemma. On the one hand, in explaining how the forms of external things exist in us whenever we apprehend, enjoy, and evaluate external objects based on sensory information, he fails to explain why these forms are also non-spatiotemporal ideas in the divine mind. On the other hand, in explaining why there are ideas of all actual and possible beings in the divine mind beyond space and time, he fails to explain how these same ideas can ever exist in us. Understandably, we can be left with the impression that Bonaventure is simply reading Christian theology into the workings of our senses. He appears to provide no independent and coherent motivation for his claim that we can see God in the human sensory process, but only a confusing and unstable mixture of Platonic and Aristotelian notions.

I believe there is more to Bonaventure's view here than meets the eye. In approaching the text of any speculative thinker, Scholastic or otherwise, it is important to step back from the words on the page and try to engage at the deepest level the thoughts the author is expressing. Such stepping back requires us to do some deep thinking ourselves in order to illuminate in the best possible light the position the author is developing. We must strike flint to ignite fire. With this advice in mind, let us return to Bonaventure's description of the human sensory process.

Suppose I am looking at the full moon in the night sky. In seeing this external object, I plainly recognize the existence of such a thing to be possible since it is right there in the sky over me! But even if I were to learn that the moon I think I am seeing no longer exists by the time my eye receives the visual information transmitted from it, or even if I were to learn that what I'm seeing is really an optical illusion of a moon that has never actually existed, nonetheless I would continue to recognize the logical possibility of the full moon existing as an external object. With Aristotle, we may say that what persuades me of this possibility is the fact that the visual properties of a possibly existing full moon exist non-substantially in my sensory experience of what appears to be a full moon in the night sky—properties which may or may not be exhibited by any actual external object. In particular, I understand the roundness of the full moon independently of whether this roundness exists in an external object or merely in my mind. These observations suggest that the logical possibility of the full moon existing as an external object amounts to the fact that roundness (and other sensible properties characteristic of a full moon) exists in a mode that is ontologically neutral between roundness existing in the full moon as external object and roundness existing merely in my mind. More generally, the logical possibility of an external object with some property P amounts to the fact that P exists in a mode that is ontologically neutral between real external existence and existence merely in some human mind (or in the mind of some other intelligent being in the universe). I will call this *the Possibility Principle.*

The Possibility Principle applies to other sensible properties, including ones like being square which cannot exist together with roundness in the same external object. For example, the logically possible existence of a square block on the floor of my office amounts to the fact that being square exists in a mode that is ontologically neutral between existing in a real block, in which case the possibility is also actual, and existing merely in my mind or the mind of some other intelligent creature, in which case the possibility isn't actual. Roundness and being square can both exist in the same mind; I understand both what it is for something to be round and what it is for something to be square. However, roundness and being square cannot exist simultaneously in the same external object; for example, it is impossible for the table in my kitchen to be round and square at the same time.

Let us now shift our attention to the limiting situation in which there is absolutely no universe of material things, no space, and no time. Such a situation might have obtained before the origin of the universe in the Big Bang. Or, according to some cosmologists, it might eventually obtain beyond some point in the distant future when the entire universe collapses into nothing. In either version of the limiting situation, it is logically possible for there to be round external objects. Otherwise, there never could be or there never could have been round external objects. The latter claim is obviously false. There actually are round external objects like the coins in my pocket, so the existence of round external objects is logically possible. Applying the Possibility Principle, it follows that roundness exists in an ontologically neutral mode in the limiting situation. The same kind of argument establishes that in the limiting situation it is logically possible for there to be square objects. Applying the Possibility Principle again, it follows that being square also exists in an ontologically neutral mode in the limiting situation. Hence both roundness and being square coexist in an ontologically neutral mode in the limiting situation.

How can roundness and being square coexist in the limiting situation? Clearly roundness and being square cannot coexist in that or any other situation by roundness and being square existing simultaneously in the same external object. Moreover, roundness and being square cannot coexist in the limiting situation by roundness existing in one external object and being square existing in a different external object, because in the limiting situation there are absolutely *no* external objects. Roundness and being square also cannot coexist in the limiting situation by simultaneous propagation through a medium, since there is no light, air, or other natural substance through which sensory information can be transmitted.

The plausible way for roundness and being square to coexist is for them to exist in the mind of someone who understands both what it is for something to be round and what it is for something to be square. Yet in the limiting situation, not only are there no external material objects, there also are no human minds and no minds of any other intelligent beings in the universe either. There is absolutely no universe. If roundness and being square coexist in an ontologically neutral mode in the limiting situation—which they do, given (1) the Possibility Principle, (2) the logically possible existence in the limiting situation of round external objects, and (3) the equally logically possible existence in the limiting situation of square external objects—only one option remains: even if there is absolutely no universe of space, time, human minds, and things, there is a divine mind in which roundness and being square coexist in an ontologically neutral mode because the divine mind understands both what it is for something to be round and what it is for something to be square. Therefore, there exists a non-spatiotemporal divine mind containing divine ideas of round beings, square beings, and of every other possible being. These divine ideas exist in us too insofar as we recognize the logically possible existence of external things based on sensory information we receive.

On the interpretation developed in the last few paragraphs, Bonaventure's case for claiming that our senses contain divine ideas whenever we perceive external objects is a *proof by constructive elimination*: in the limiting situation where there is no material universe, the co-possibility of external objects with incompatible sensory properties requires the ontologically neutral co-existence of these same properties in the limiting situation. These properties don't coexist in something spatiotemporal and external to our minds because there is nothing spatiotemporal in the limiting situation. They don't coexist in any human mind because there are no human minds in the limiting situation either. Bonaventure combines the remainder from both options to arrive at his answer: in the limiting situation incompatible sensory properties coexist non-spatiotemporally in a non-human mind that is external to our minds. That is, the properties coexist as ideas in the divine mind, just as they coexist in our minds when we understand roundness and being square, or whenever perceive a round external object over here and a square object over there.

Bonaventure's answer can also be understood as a solution to a puzzle in Platonic metaphysics. Recall that Platonic Forms are held to coexist in an abstract "third realm" beyond human minds, space, and time. In particular, the Form of roundness and the Form of being square coexist there. How? Presumably these Forms would coexist there without themselves being round and square entities, respectively; otherwise, it is no clearer how round and square entities could coexist in the same "third realm" than in the same spatiotemporal location.[19] But *how* does the Form of being round exist

19. On a possible variant of Plato's theory, some Forms are self-predicable whereas other Forms aren't; for example the Form the Good is itself good whereas the Form of being a horse isn't itself a horse. The Forms of roundness and being a square might be like the Form of being a horse rather than the Form of the Good in that they aren't self-predicable. Readers interested in these and related issues may wish to consult Malcolm, *Plato on Self-Predication of Forms*.

in the "third realm" without itself being round, and how does the Form of being square exist there too without itself being square? The problem disappears if the Form of roundness and the Form of being square exist in the "third realm" in a way that is similar to how roundness and being square exist non-substantially in our minds. Our minds aren't round and square merely because we understand roundness and being square. But then, rather than Platonic Forms, there are divine ideas; and rather than existing in a mysterious "third realm," these ideas exist eternally in the divine mind.

Bonaventure's case for our sensory experiences containing divine ideas relies heavily on the Possibility Principle. Perhaps that principle is objectionable as an explanation of logical possibility. However, in the absence of some alternative explanation it is difficult to see why—especially given the expansive understanding of being and the basically Aristotelian epistemology shared by Bonaventure and many of his medieval contemporaries. Intuitively, the logical possibility of a chiliagon the size of Pluto "is" something, though not something actual. If it were absolutely nothing then all non-actual logical possibilities would be absolutely nothing and hence exactly the same, which they aren't. Moreover, the logical possibility of a chiliagon the size of Pluto includes the property of being a chiliagon which we can understand whether or not it is actually instantiated in reality. Thus the logical possibility does seem to involve the ontologically neutral existence of the property. More cautiously, then, we may say given his metaphysical and epistemological starting points, both of which we have seen have intuitive appeal, Bonaventure can motivate the Possibility Principle and then apply it to make a strong case for our sensory experiences containing divine ideas whenever we perceive external objects. We hasten to add the proviso that the expansive understanding of being and the Aristotle-inspired epistemology both deserve more careful scrutiny.

Lastly, we began this chapter by distinguishing images from mere vestiges: unlike vestiges, images literally depict God. Since a depiction is distinct from what it depicts, so is an image. Yet the divine ideas which, according to Bonaventure, exist in us whenever we perceive external objects with our senses *are* God, or at least they are elements of God's wisdom that, taken in its totality, is one in being with God. Since these ideas aren't distinct from God, it seems that they can't really depict Him and hence aren't really His images.

Bonaventure might reply that a divine idea existing in you whenever you perceive an external object (or even when you merely seem to) is only one among infinitely many divine ideas existing eternally in God. The totality of these ideas comprises a perfect likeness, the Eternal Art of the Son, that is an ontologically distinct person from what it depicts, the Father, while remaining one in being with it. Thus unlike a mere vestige, any divine idea in you when you perceive an external object is contained in a perfect likeness or depiction of God that conforms to some discrimination of God's being. Like a tile in a mosaic, a divine idea in you is part of a larger image of divinity. What remains to be explained is why the totality of divine ideas constitutes a divine person, or whether such a notion even makes sense. These are among the matters we shall examine in subsequent chapters.

Discussion Questions

(1) On the Aristotelian epistemology of perception, should we understand the form that exists substantially in a particular elm and non-substantially in my eye when I see the elm as also existing substantially in every other elm of the same species, so that there is literally one and only one substantial form common to all these elms?

  (a) If so, then why aren't elms sharing an identical substantial form identical themselves?

  (b) If not, then what is the relation between the non-identical substantial forms in different elms of the same species?

(2) If the Son is an ontologically distinct person from the Father, then how can they be one in being?

(3) If there is a multiplicity of divine ideas, then how can God be "utterly simple," as Bonaventure maintains in agreement with other Scholastic philosopher-theologians?[20]

---

20. See, for example ibid., 97–101.

FOUR

Necessity and Divinity

Bonaventure argues that at the first stage of the soul's journey into God we see God "through the mirror" of external material objects which exhibit the power, wisdom, and goodness of the First Principle by exhibiting trans-categorical characteristics. He argues that at the second stage we see God "in the mirror" of our sensory experiences informed by eternally existing divine ideas whenever we perceive external objects. "Now in the third stage," Bonaventure tells us, "we enter into our very selves; and, as it were, leaving the outer court, we should strive to see God through a mirror in the sanctuary, that is, in the forward area of the tabernacle."[1] Specifically, Bonaventure argues that the human soul possesses three powers or faculties—memory, intellect, and will—which are vestiges not only of God as transcendent First Principle but

1. Bonaventure, *Soul's Journey into God*, 79.

of God as a Trinity of divine Persons: Father, Son, and Holy Spirit.

Before we take up this ambitious agenda, a methodological worry needs to be aired. We saw how Bonaventure's proof by exclusion is intended to provide anyone with rational warrant for believing that a First Principle exists, even someone who doesn't already believe in the God of Christian orthodoxy. Extending the same strategy to the Trinity is problematic. For then there would have to be reasons for believing that God exists as Father, Son, and Holy Spirit available to anyone independently of faith. However, Christian orthodoxy, including the Scholastic tradition to which Bonaventure belongs, teaches the doctrine of the Trinity to be a truth we cannot derive on the basis of reason alone; instead, it must be revealed to us by God Himself through faith. Human reason may shed some light on this mystery by showing that such a thing is not utterly absurd or impossible. Yet human reason by itself cannot bring us to assent to the Trinitarian mystery or to comprehend it fully. Only faith can. If Bonaventure is offering a philosophical proof for the Trinity, then contrary to Christian orthodoxy and his own intellectual tradition he is treating it as a purely rational truth rather than a revealed truth. On the other hand, if he is *not* offering a philosophical proof for the Trinity based on an analysis of our mental faculties, then it is obscure why he thinks these faculties are vestiges of the triune God.

Textually, there is some indication that Bonaventure does not mean to offer a purely philosophical proof for the existence of the Trinity. Near the end of his third chapter he comments:

> And thus our mind, illumined and flooded by such
> brilliance, unless it is blind can be led through itself
> to contemplate that Eternal Light. The radiation
> and contemplation of this Light lifts up the wise
> in wonder; and on the contrary *it leads to confu-*
> *sion the fools who do not believe so that they may*
> *understand.*[2]

Expressed in less pejorative terms, this passage implies that
although any reasonable person, even a religious skeptic,
can discover the existence of a transcendent First Principle
from clear signs in the material universe, someone cannot
understand how our mental powers reflect the triune nature
of the First Principle unless she already believes the doctrine
of the Trinity. Hence in the course of Bonaventure's account
of the third stage we should expect a shift away from neutral
propositions of philosophy toward propositions that can be
seriously entertained only by those who have faith. To understand this shift, we now turn to the details of Bonaventure's
argument.

Parallel to his description of how the seven trans-
categorical characteristics of things in the material universe
exhibit God's power, wisdom, and goodness, Bonaventure
describes how our mental powers of memory, intellect,
and choice possess features indicating some aspect of God.
According to Bonaventure, each power possesses three
such features, for a total of nine divinity-indicating features.
Furthermore, "These powers [of memory, intellect, and will]
lead us to the most blessed Trinity itself in view of their order, origin, and interrelatedness."[3] Thus our evaluation of

2. Ibid., 85, emphasis added.
3. Ibid., 84.

Bonaventure's overall argument must determine not only whether each feature really indicates some aspect of divinity but also whether the tripartite structure of the human mind itself reflects the triune nature of the First Principle. We begin by examining Bonaventure's reasons for thinking that each feature he describes indicates some aspect of divinity.

Memory:[4] Events in the past, the present, or the future can eventually be retained in memory. When you were ten years old, events prior to that time (e.g., your learning to ride a bicycle), events contemporaneous with that time (e.g., your tenth birthday party), and events future to that time (e.g., getting your driver's license) are all eventually retained in your adult memory. Moreover, *any* given event in time has the potential to be retained in the memory of some human being or other; for example, if someone had witnessed a Tyrannosaurus attacking a Brontosaurus millions of years ago, she could have retained that episode in her memory. Since the same human faculty of memory is exercised in each of these cases, any given event has the potential to be present to the same human faculty of memory by being remembered by someone or other. The potential retention of any given event to the faculty of human memory implies the actual presence of any given event to something not in time but in eternity—namely, God.[5] Therefore, human memory is an image of divine eternity.

4. See ibid., 80–81.

5. A useful analogy of things in time being present to something not in time but in eternity is that of a student in 1600, a student in 1867, and a student in 2010 each calculating that 5 is the positive square root of 25, where 5 and 25 are abstract objects beyond space and time but potentially present to students calculating the positive square root of 25 at any time in human history.

The last step of this argument is shaky. From the fact that any event has the potential to be remembered by someone or other, it obviously doesn't follow that every event is actually remembered by someone or other, and hence that every event is actually retained in the faculty of human memory shared by the various humans who remember these events. And if it doesn't follow that all events are actually present to a type of temporal thinking—namely, human memory—then even less does it follow that all events are actually present to a type of non-temporal thinking—namely, eternal divine cognition. To anticipate a bit, Bonaventure might be saying that a full analysis (*plene resolvens*) of human memory as something in time and potentially present to all times naturally leads to the idea of something not in time and actually present to all times which is only approximated by human memory. However, even if we can form the idea of such an ideal eternal thing, so far we have no reason to think that this idea corresponds to something that really exists, any more than we have reason to think that the idea we can form of perfect judge only approximated by human judges corresponds to a perfect judge in reality.

The other two features of human memory that Bonaventure describes are its retaining concepts of simple quantities and its retaining axioms or first principles employed in the sciences. No one teaches us about mathematical points, instants, and units by showing us such entities in nature, for there are none. Yet when presented with these concepts we immediately grasp them, suggesting that we retrieve information already in our minds rather than receive new information. Bonaventure takes these "simple forms"[6] of basic

6. Ibid., 81.

mathematical quantities to reflect the simplicity of God as a non-composite being. Though he doesn't spell it out, perhaps his implicit argument parallels the proof by exclusion at the first stage: the fundamental simplicity shared by mathematical points, instants, and units can't be reduced to the simplicity of any one of these conceptual entities; therefore, it must be the transcendent simplicity of something neither in the material universe nor merely in the human mind. In the case of scientific axioms and first principles, we not only assent to them as soon as they are put to us but we also recognize that they cannot be otherwise and so must be immutably true.[7] From our recognition of their immutability, Bonaventure infers that "the memory has an unchangeable light present to itself in which it remembers immutable truths" (ibid.)—namely, the immutable God who illuminates our minds.

Below we shall return to the immutability of axioms and principles in connection with the intellect, since Bonaventure also regards the necessary propositions and inferences the intellect grasps as immutable truths. For now, we may observe that his implicit argument for a transcendent, divine simplicity differs in a crucial respect from his earlier argument for a

---

7. Bonaventure's examples of axioms—"On any matter, one must affirm or deny," "Every whole is greater than its part" (ibid., 80)—may be contested or rejected as false. For example, mathematical intuitionists maintain that we may neither affirm nor deny that 8 occurs infinitely many times in the decimal expansion of pi without a proof one way or the other; and the cardinality of the set of all natural numbers is not greater than but equals the cardinality of the set of all odd natural numbers that is part of it. Nevertheless, the substance of Bonaventure's point remains, in that there are at least some axiomatic propositions—e.g., a statement and its negation cannot be true simultaneously—which are so obvious that we assent to them immediately and recognize that they can't be otherwise than true.

transcendent power, wisdom, and goodness. The triple property of power, wisdom, and goodness is really exhibited by material things in virtue of their equally real trans-categorical characteristics, making it possible to infer that this triple property is also a real attribute of something not in the material universe. But the fundamental simplicity of mathematical points, instants, and units isn't exhibited by any real things in the universe because there are no such entities. Unless fundamental simplicity is a property equally exhibited by real immanent things, there is no argument from this premise to the conclusion that the same property is also exhibited by some real transcendent thing. No less than a frictionless plane in physics, the simplicity of mathematical points, instants, and units remains at a purely conceptual level.

Intellect:[8] Bonaventure distinguishes two kinds of understanding in the human intellect: understanding the terms in a definition, and understanding the necessity of certain propositions and inferences. The former kind of understanding, Bonaventure argues, leads to God via a full analysis (*plene resolvens*) of definitional terms. For example, *human* is defined as *rational animal*. We cannot understand this definition unless we understand the more universal term *animal*, which in turn requires that we understand the even more universal term *organism* used in the definition of *animal* and the maximally universal term *being* used in the definition of *organism* as *living corporeal being*. Indeed, our understanding of any definition requires that we understand *being*; even *nothing* is defined as the total absence of *being*. Moreover, we recognize that many beings are defective, incomplete, or at least limited

8. See ibid., 81–82.

in some respect; even a totally healthy organism at the height of its powers doesn't live forever, unsusceptible to any weakness. Bonaventure argues that since full understanding of a defective, incomplete, or limited being consists in appreciating how it approximates perfect, complete, and unlimited being, the human intellect "is aided by a knowledge of the Being which is most pure, most actual, most complete and absolute, which is unqualified and Eternal Being."[9] Unfortunately, the same kind of objection against taking human memory to be an image of divine eternity can also be raised here: fully understanding a being as limited may presuppose that we have an idea of unlimited being, but it doesn't follow that our idea corresponds to anything in reality.

The nerve of Bonaventure's case for identifying the human intellect as a vestige of God, I suggest, is the notion of necessity. Although he distinguishes our understanding of necessary propositions from our understanding of necessary inferences, Bonaventure maintains that both kinds of necessity have the same explanation. A necessary proposition is such that the intellect "knows that this truth cannot be otherwise; therefore, it knows that this truth is unchangeable."[10] For example, the definitional proposition "Bachelors are adult unmarried males" is an immutable necessary truth. Given their immutable truth, the axioms and first principles comprehended by the intellect and retained in the memory also count as necessary propositions. A necessary inference holds between a conclusion and one or more premises from which the conclusion must follow. Bonaventure's example is the necessary inference from "A man is running" to "The [same]

9. Ibid., 82.
10. Ibid.

man is moving";[11] another example is the necessary inference from "If Marie went to town then Marie visited Jules" and "Marie went to town" to "Marie visited Jules." The connection between the premise(s) and conclusion in a necessary inference is no less immutable than the truth of a necessary proposition.

What is the metaphysical basis for the immutability of necessary propositions and inferences? Not material things, Bonaventure reasons, since material things are mutable and contingent.[12] He also denies that anything like an idea in our minds provides a metaphysical basis for the immutability of necessary propositions and inferences. Bonaventure's compressed argument seems to be that without any external correlate, the idea in our minds would be a fiction, so that what counts as a necessary truth or inference would be decided by us—just as it is up to a storyteller whether all humans are necessarily animals (e.g., in the story, she may decide that some humans turn out to be plants) and whether "Markus is an animal" necessarily follows from "Markus is human" (i.e., not if he's a plant human!). Since necessary truths and inferences aren't decided by us, their immutability isn't based merely upon our own ideas. Bonaventure concludes that their immutability ultimately has its source in "some light which

11. Ibid.

12. Some philosophers like Avicenna and Spinoza hold that material things aren't mutable and contingent but unfold necessarily. Bonaventure might challenge these philosophers to provide a precise description of actual material things, events, and processes making it clear how they unfold no less necessarily than the chain of inferences in a deductive proof (logical determination) or than a line of falling dominos (causal determination).

shines forth in an absolutely unchanging way":[13] namely, the divine Light. The immutability of a necessary proposition consists in God's unchangingly thinking the divine ideas constituting it; the immutability of a necessary inference consists in God's unchangingly inferring its conclusion from its premises, which is a relation between divine ideas in the Eternal Art.[14]

On this interpretation, Bonaventure is offering a metaphysical explanation of necessity. The explanation assumes that the necessity of a necessary proposition or a necessary inference consists in its immutability. Bonaventure then explains the immutability of necessary propositions and inferences in terms of the immutability of divine thinking. But is necessity the same as immutability? There are good reasons to think not, since something can be immutable without being necessary. For example, God eternally knows that Socrates is bald. Hence this divine knowledge is immutable. Yet Socrates' being bald, and thus God's knowledge of Socrates' being bald, isn't necessary but contingent because Socrates might not have been bald. Moreover, consider any past event, such as Caesar's crossing the Rubicon. Like all past events, this event is immutable because it cannot change once it has happened. However, Caesar's crossing the Rubicon isn't necessary but contingent. Thus necessity, including the necessity of necessary propositions and inferences, consists in more than immutability. But then merely explaining the *immutability* of necessary propositions and inferences in terms of the immutability of divine thinking fails to explain the *necessity* of these

13. Ibid.
14. See ibid., 82–83.

propositions and inferences, and Bonaventure's main case for identifying the human intellect as a vestige of God collapses.[15]

There may be more to Bonaventure's reflections on necessity than this failed explanation, however. Before we dig deeper, let us consider what Bonaventure regards as divinity-indicating features of our third mental faculty, and also why he thinks that the tripartite structure of the human mind itself is a vestige of the Trinity.

Choice:[16] Bonaventure focuses on situations in which we make a deliberate moral choice. For example, I may choose not to steal a horse I want but to work until I earn enough money to buy it from the owner. My choosing carefully requires that I deliberate about what it is better for me to do: steal the horse or earn enough money to buy it. Since one thing is better for me than another thing only if the first thing more closely resembles what is best for me, there is something that is best for me: namely, my highest good, which is my eternal life with God. Furthermore, I choose not to steal the

15. Could Bonaventure still appeal to divine immutability to explain the immutability, though not the necessity, of necessary propositions and inferences? The prospects are dim if, as in the case of Caesar's crossing the Rubicon and other past events, we can make sense of immutability independently of divinity: perhaps the past can't change because there is no such thing as backward causation, which applies equally to immutable propositions and inferences given that what happens later can't change them. Note that Bonaventure relates the immutability of necessary propositions and inferences to the immutability of the divine Light that floods the human intellect when we consider them. Since immutability provides no explanation of necessity, I have avoided appealing to divine illumination in an explanation of the necessity of necessary propositions and inferences. Nonetheless, readers may wish to consider what constructive role, if any, divine illumination plays in Bonaventure's epistemology.

16. See ibid., 83–84.

horse because I judge in accordance with the moral law that stealing is wrong. We don't make moral judgments about this and other moral laws; rather, this and other moral laws make it possible for us to make moral judgments in the first place. Hence these laws are higher than our minds. Since whatever is higher than our minds has its origin in God, it follows that the laws according to which we make moral judgments are divine laws. Finally, I choose to earn enough money to buy the horse because I want it, and I want the horse because having it will make me happy. Since my happiness is good for me, my choice involves my desire for what is good for me. And since something is good for me only if it resembles to some degree what is best for me, as before it follows that there is something best for me: again, my highest good as my eternal life with God.

The arguments from deliberation and desire to the existence of the highest good both contain the premise that if something is good or better for me then there is something that is best for me. This common premise requires that we think of goodness as comparable to resemblance: X is good for me only if X resembles the highest good Z to some degree; and Y is better for me than X only if Y more closely resembles Z than X does.[17] But what if goodness is a positive intensity rather than a relational property involving resemblance to an exemplar? Then something could be good for me and one thing could be better for me than another thing without all these things resembling in varying degrees something that is best for me, just as an object can have a size and one object can

17. As Bonaventure puts it, "No one, therefore, knows whether this is better than that unless he knows that it bears a greater resemblance to the best" (ibid., 83).

have a larger size than another object without all these objects resembling in varying degrees some largest object. Perhaps the influence of Platonic metaphysics on Bonaventure makes it natural for him to construe goodness as involving resemblance to the highest good as an exemplar. But he doesn't justify this Platonic construal of goodness or rule out the alternative construal of goodness as an infinitely increasing positive intensity, so that the common premise is left hanging and the arguments in which it figures are unpersuasive.

As it stands, Bonaventure's argument from moral laws to divinity is equally unsuccessful. Consider an analogy: the rules of chess are higher than our minds, in that we don't make judgments about the rules while playing chess but the rules make it possible for us to play chess. Something is a chess move if and only if it conforms to the rules of the game, just as something is a moral act if and only if it conforms to moral laws; we can imagine people playing according to different rules or acting according to different laws, but then they wouldn't be playing *chess* or acting *morally*. From the fact that the rules of chess are higher than our minds in the aforementioned sense, does it follow that these rules have a divine origin? No. Although the rules of chess regulate our chess-playing behavior, nevertheless they either evolved from human game-playing practices until someone wrote them down, or they emerged from human thinking when somebody devised a new game and called it chess. We might say that the possibility of such rules eventually evolving or emerging is inherent in human thinking, symbol-making, and playing. But then, from the fact that moral laws are higher than our minds it doesn't follow that these laws have a divine origin either. Instead, such laws may grow out of human traditions, practices, and thinking because the possibility of such laws evolving or emerging is inherent in being human. Perhaps there is some kind of necessity involved in moral laws, from which Bonaventure might infer that they are vestiges of God. Yet we have seen that Bonaventure's apparent argument from necessity to divinity—and hence any argument from the necessity of moral laws to divinity—is unsatisfactory.

Bonaventure completes his account of the third stage of the soul's journey by arguing that the tripartite structure of the human mind consisting of memory, intellect, and choice or will reflects the Trinity as three divine persons in one divine nature.[18] When you understand something, such as that spring has arrived, the mental "word" or concept *spring* comes forth from your memory where it is retained even when you aren't thinking about spring. Bonaventure regards the coming forth of a concept from memory to mirror the eternal coming forth or begetting of the Son as perfect likeness from the Father. Furthermore, your understanding that spring has arrived may "breathe forth" your love of spring. Bonaventure takes such love, which your will has only on the basis of your understanding of what spring is and thus on the concept *spring* coming forth from you memory, to mirror the breathing forth of the Holy Spirit as the mutual Love of the Father and the Son. Bonaventure also takes the co-occurrence of Paul's memory, intellect, and will in the single substance that is Paul to reflect the co-occurrence of the three divine Persons in a single substance that is God.

Bonaventure's Trinitarian argument raises a number of interesting theological questions. Is the human vestige of the

18. See ibid., 84.

Son simply the fact that for you to possess a specific concept essentially depends on that concept being retained in your memory? Or is it the fact that the concept actually comes forth from your memory in a particular act of understanding? (e.g., "Spring is here" sincerely uttered by you on the first spring day of 2010.) Similarly, is the human vestige of the Spirit the abiding love of spring you have even when you aren't manifesting it? Or is it you manifesting your love of spring in a particular act of love (e.g., "How I love spring!" sincerely uttered by you on the first spring day of 2010).

Aside from these questions, there is a more fundamental problem with Bonaventure's argument. For the tripartite structure of the human mind to be a mirror "through which" we see the Trinity, there must be a full analysis (*plene resolvens*) of human memory, intellect, and choice showing that three Persons exist in the transcendent First Principle. If this full analysis is like that of definitional terms, then a complete understanding of these faculties either presupposes or naturally leads to some idea of the Trinity. Yet it is difficult to see how a complete understanding of our memory, intellect, and choice presupposes an idea of the Trinity used to define or otherwise elucidate these faculties.[19] Even if it did, the idea of the Trinity might not correspond to anything in reality. If, on the other hand, the full analysis of our three mental faculties is supposed to be like the proof by exclusion described in chapter 2, it seems that the proof can't even get off the ground. For each mental faculty would have to exhibit a triple person-

19. If the First Principle is a Trinity, then perhaps a complete understanding of our faculties would note similarities between them and the triune divine nature. But then we must already know what the argument purports to show: namely, that the First Principle is a Trinity.

hood that cannot be reduced to the triple personhood of any one faculty, and therefore transcends our minds. But obviously neither our memory, nor our intellect, nor our power of choice is a *person*, let alone three of them!

From our study of Bonaventure's treatise so far, we have encountered two possible readings of what he means by a full analysis. On the first reading, a full analysis brings out the most basic ideas involved in a complete understanding of something (*being* in the case of animals, humans, and indeed anything whatsoever). On the second reading, a full analysis is a proof by exclusion from things in the universe exhibiting some property to something not in the universe possessing that same property as an attribute. These different readings create a logical space for attributing a number of possible arguments to the Seraphic Doctor. Reading full analysis in the first way, we see that Bonaventure's arguments aren't very good. Reading full analysis in the second way, in chapter 2 we saw that Bonaventure provides a prima facie plausible proof by exclusion for the existence of a First Principle. In this chapter, we noted that a proof by exclusion for the real simplicity of the First Principle based on the simplicity exhibited by mathematical points, instants, and units doesn't succeed because such ideal simple quantities aren't real. Yet necessity, in the form of necessary propositions and necessary inferences, is certainly real, not ideal or fictitious. We may then wonder whether there is a plausible proof by exclusion from propositions and inferences exhibiting necessity to something not in the universe possessing this same necessity. How might such a proof proceed?

As a medieval thinker Bonaventure has a traditional Aristotelian conception of logic. Modern symbolic logic pioneered by Gottlob Frege, Bertrand Russell, and others isn't even a blip on his intellectual radar screen. Yet Bonaventure does appreciate how axioms, inferences, and conclusions derived from axioms via inferences all differ. His sketchy remarks imply a considerably broader understanding of these notions than the kind found in contemporary logic textbooks. For example Bonaventure doesn't limit axioms to truth-functional tautologies, such as all instances of the schema $\lceil P \rightarrow (Q \rightarrow P) \rceil$, but takes them to include definitional truths as well as "the principles and axioms of the sciences."[20] Thus "Bachelors are unmarried adult males," the metaphysical principle that something cannot cause itself, the color exclusion principle that something cannot simultaneously be one color all over and another color all over, the Peano axioms for arithmetic, and the axiom of extension in set theory would presumably all count as axioms by Bonaventure's lights. His understanding of necessary inferences is similarly broad, covering not only rules like modus ponens ("A proposition of the form Q may be inferred from propositions of the form P and $\lceil P \rightarrow Q \rceil$") but also rules like "A proposition of the form $\lceil X$ is moving$\rceil$ may be inferred from a proposition of the form $\lceil X$ is running$\rceil$ where X is replaced by a name." Conclusions following from necessary axioms via necessary rules of inference are equally necessary.[21] Bonaventure does not have some inchoate idea

20. Ibid., 80.

21. For Bonaventure, necessary rules of inference also license inferences from contingent premises, which thus aren't axioms, to contingent conclusions. Thus they are rules "according to which things are mutually oriented and related to one another because they are represented in the Eternal Art" (ibid., 83)—including contingent things both actual and merely possible. For his philosophical and theological purposes, Bonaventure focuses on *necessary* conclusions drawn

of a monolithic formal system encompassing all of human thinking; the idea of a formal system is foreign to him. His conception of necessary axioms, inferences, and conclusions is more fluid: throughout our thinking, there are manifold discursive practices in which we draw necessary conclusions from necessary axioms via necessary inference rules.

Implicit in Bonaventure's recognition of how axioms, inference rules, and conclusions differ is the importance of not conflating them.[22] Conclusions obviously aren't the same as axioms or inference rules but are ultimately derived from the former by means of the latter. Inference rules also differ from axioms. Otherwise, we would never be able to infer any conclusions from axioms; we could only add more and more axioms, ad infinitum.[23] It now looks as if a full analysis of the necessity of axioms, inferences, and conclusions yields a proof by exclusion for the existence of a transcendent necessity. Axioms, inference rules, and conclusions occurring in the universe (by occurring in our manifold practices and disciplines) all exhibit the property of being necessary. If this property were identical with either being an axiom, being an inference rule, or the being a conclusion, then either an

---

from *necessary* premises (axioms) via *necessary* rules of inference. (Unless otherwise indicated, by "conclusions" I shall mean necessary conclusions.)

22. Bonaventure sometimes blurs the distinction between inference rules and axioms; for example, he expresses one of his inference rules as the proposition "If a man is running, the [same] man is moving" (ibid., 82). To keep the distinction clearly in mind, in my exposition I have expressed this and other inference rules somewhat anachronistically. Nevertheless, at the end of this chapter I will suggest that Bonaventure's blurring might have a theological point.

23. Such is the lesson of Carroll, "What Achilles Said to the Tortoise."

axiom's necessity consists in its being an inference rule or a conclusion, or else an inference rule's necessity consists in its being an axiom or conclusion, or else a conclusion's necessity consists in its being an axiom or inference rule. Given that axioms, inference rules, and conclusions are all distinct, any such result is absurd. Therefore, the property of being necessary exhibited by axioms, by inference rules, and by conclusions does not consist in being an axiom, an inference rule, or a conclusion. Nonetheless, it is a real property. To be a real property distinct from being any of these necessary things in the universe, the property of being necessary must also be a real attribute of something not in the universe. Therefore, there exists something not in the universe of which the property of being necessary is an attribute.

As with Bonaventure's earlier proof by exclusion, objections might be raised against the current proof. One could agree that necessity is a property distinct from being an axiom, an inference rule, or a conclusion, but disagree that necessity is an attribute of something transcendent. Instead, necessity may be defined in terms of "possible worlds."[24] Axioms and conclusions following from them via inference rules are necessary because these propositions are true in all possible worlds. A given inference rule R is necessary because the following proposition is true in all possible worlds: "Any possible world in which R's premises are true is also a possible world in which R's conclusion is true." However, Bonaventure might reasonably wonder what it means to say that the relevant propositions are "true in all possible worlds." Is this

24. The *loci classici* of much contemporary possible-worlds theory are Lewis, *Counterfactuals* and Kripke, *Naming and Necessity*. Lewis develops his version of "modal realism" in his *On the Plurality of Worlds*.

just a fancy way of saying that axioms, inferences rules, and conclusions are *necessary*? If so, then talk of "possible worlds" fails to describe a property of necessity that is distinct from being an axiom, an inference rule, or a conclusion and we are back where we started. Are "possible worlds" creatures of human imagination? If they are, then why isn't any necessity explained in terms of "possible worlds" equally fictitious? Perhaps possible worlds are just as real as our own world but inaccessible to us apart from our ability to conceive of them. Then there is a plurality of possible worlds constituting something like a necessary structure undergirding all of reality. If so, then Bonaventure can be expected to riposte that the necessity exhibited by axioms, inference rules, conclusions, and possible worlds too is not identical with any of these entities but is a real attribute of something transcending them all. These are difficult issues which we cannot resolve here. Suffice it to say that, at least for the time being, this line of objection against Bonaventure's proof remains inconclusive.

A potentially more serious objection challenges Bonaventure's assumption that there is a property of being necessary common to axioms, inference rules, and conclusions. Just as various games such as golf, tennis, solitaire, and curling have no common property in virtue of which they are all games, neither do the axioms, inference rules, nor conclusions occurring in our manifold discursive practices share a single property in virtue of which they are all necessary. There are merely "family resemblances" among these modes of necessity: axioms are like conclusions yet unlike inference rules in that they are propositions; inference rules are like axioms yet unlike conclusions in that they are starting points for deductions; conclusions are inference rules yet unlike axioms in that they are fewer in number (often just one) in a typical deduction.[25] If there is no property of being necessary common to axioms, inference rules, and conclusions, then a proof by exclusion that this "property" is also an attribute of something transcendent is a non-starter. To the extent that we can give any clear content to the expressions "being necessary" and "necessity" as Bonaventure applies them to various features of our manifold discursive practices, our reflecting on the family resemblances among these features should dissuade us from starting down the garden path of the proposed "proof."

Suppose that Bonaventure is wrong and that what he describes as necessary axioms, inference rules, and conclusions exhibit only overlapping resemblances rather than a common property of being necessary. In our evaluation of Bonaventure's argument from moral laws to divinity, we saw how the eventual evolution or emergence of moral laws, chess rules, and other norms regulating human behavior is a possibility inherent in human traditions, practices, and thinking. Presumably the same is true for Bonaventure's necessary axioms, inference rules, and conclusions even if they do not exhibit a common property of being necessary: the eventual evolution or emergence of axioms, inference rules, and conclusions characterized merely by overlapping resemblances is a possibility inherent in human discursive practices, which themselves are a possibility inherent in being human. To say

25. Ludwig Wittgenstein introduces the notion of "family resemblances" as a kind of unity among different things of the same kind (e.g., games or linguistic practices) lacking a common property in virtue of which they are things of that kind. See Wittgenstein, *Philosophical Investigations*, sections 65–71.

that the evolution or emergence of such axioms, inference rules, and conclusions is a possibility *inherent* in being human is tantamount to saying that it is *necessarily* possible for creatures of the kind we are to develop discursive practices featuring axioms, inference rules, and conclusions with overlapping resemblances. Therefore, even if these three things don't share the property of being necessary, they are necessarily possible in the aforementioned sense.

Using a notion we first encountered in chapter 2, we may now ask what the real basis is for such things to be, if not inevitable, then at least necessarily possible. To put the point vividly, in the limiting situation described in chapter 3 where there is no universe of material things, space, or time, in virtue of what is it necessarily possible for there to be creatures of the kind we are who eventually develop discursive practices featuring axioms, inference rules, and conclusions with only overlapping resemblances? Bonaventure's answer is that even in the limiting situation where there is nothing else, there is a transcendent being whose existence is necessary and who encompasses all such possibilities as ideas in its mind. These ideas, like the transcendent being whose ideas they are, exist necessarily. Hence the possibilities equated with these necessary ideas are necessarily possible. Again, the possible reply I attribute to Bonaventure in this paragraph raises difficult issues deserving further study and discussion. But at this stage we can be forgiven for thinking that there really is garden path here and for being eager to go down it further.

Let us return to the methodological worry mentioned at the beginning of this chapter. If there is a philosophical proof by exclusion from the necessity of axioms, inference rules, and conclusions to the existence of a transcendent necessity, then it seems we can know on purely rational grounds that God is a Trinity of divine Persons. For the transcendent necessity exhibited by axioms, inference rules, and conclusions is God's necessary being. Furthermore, each mode of worldly necessity mirrors a divine person within transcendent necessity. As the ultimate basis for deductions, axioms mirror the Father as the ultimate basis for the procession of the Persons. As making explicit the timeless logical connections between premises and conclusions, rules of inference mirror the timeless relations among divine ideas in the Son as Eternal Art. As following from the axioms via the inference rules, (necessary) conclusions mirror the procession of the Holy Spirit from the Father through the Son. But if human reason is sufficient to prove that God's necessary being includes three necessary divine Persons then the Trinity is a purely rational rather than a revealed truth—a consequence contrary to Christian orthodoxy.

I do not think that Bonaventure intends to establish any such hyper-rationalistic consequence. At most, he shows that the necessity exhibited by axioms, inference rules, and conclusions mirrors a transcendent necessity. Beyond that result, all we can say is that there appears to be a threefold differentiation in this transcendent necessity reflected by the different manifestations of necessity in worldly axioms, inference rules, and conclusions. For suppose we try to prove on purely rational grounds that the threefold differentiation in transcendent necessity is in fact a Trinity of divine Persons. We would then have to deduce the existence of the Father as a necessary divine person, so that we would treat his necessity like the necessity of a conclusion—which is something deduced—rather than the necessity of an axiom—which isn't deduced. But the necessity of the Father is supposedly mirrored by the necessity of non-deduced axioms, not the necessity of deduced conclusions! Similarly, we would have to deduce the existence of the Son, and hence inappropriately treat his necessity as comparable to the necessity of a conclusion, as opposed to treating it appropriately as comparable to the necessity of an inference rule. To deduce the existence of the Holy Spirit as a necessary divine person proceeding from the Father and the Son, we would first have to deduce the existence of latter two necessary divine persons, again treating what should be comparable to the necessity of axioms (the Father) and what should be comparable to the necessity of inference rules (the Son) as both comparable to the necessity of conclusions.

Therefore, the moment we set out to prove the necessary existence of three divine Persons each reflected by a mode of worldly necessity, we can never prove what we are trying to prove. The result isn't rational truth but incoherence. Without some divine revelation, perhaps clarified somewhat through the aid of human reason, we cannot know that God exists as a Trinity of Persons. At best all we can know is that there is some threefold differentiation in transcendent necessity dimly reflected by the three modes of necessity occurring in the world. Bonaventure only promises his readers that at the current stage of the soul's journey "you will be able to see God through yourself as through an image, which is to see *through a mirror in an obscure manner* [1 Cor 13:12]."[26]

At the other extreme, it might be denied that the necessity of axioms, inference rules, and conclusions deduced from the

26. Bonaventure, *Soul's Journey into God*, 80.

axioms via the inference rules reflects or mirrors the Father, Son, and Holy Spirit—at least as the Trinity is understood according to Roman Catholic teaching, which Bonaventure accepts. The criticism here is theological. The church teaches that the Father eternally begets the Son and that the Spirit eternally proceeds from the Father and the Son. The eternal procession of the Spirit from the Father and the Son might be reflected by necessary conclusions (comparable to the Spirit) eternally following from necessary axioms (comparable to the Father) via necessary inference rules (comparable to the Son as Eternal Art). Yet on this model, what reflects the eternal begetting of the Son by the Father? Bonaventure cannot say what reflects it is the necessary inference rules following from necessary axioms. Inference rules aren't deduced from axioms; rather, inference rules are what license the deduction of conclusions from axioms. Apparently, then, axioms have no logical priority over inference rules, though both axioms and inference rules have logical priority over conclusions. But unless inference rules somehow logically depend upon axioms, the relation between the two does not even dimly reflect the ontological dependence of the Son upon the Father.

I believe Bonaventure has room to maneuver around this theological criticism. Specifically, he might grant that inference rules don't logically follow from axioms. After all, unlike axioms and conclusions inference rules aren't propositions. However, it seems safe to say that if certain axioms weren't necessarily true, a given inference rule wouldn't be necessary. For example, the proposition "If Socrates is running then Socrates is moving" seems to count as an axiom on Bonaventure's view.[27] Suppose, *per impossibile*, that this proposition weren't true because it could be the case that Socrates is running without its being the case that Socrates is moving. Then in general we may not infer a proposition of the form ⌈X is moving⌉ from a proposition of the form ⌈X is running⌉, hence precluding the necessity of the associated rule of inference.

By contrast, we might continue on Bonaventure's behalf, the converse dependence does not hold. If, *per impossibile*, the above inference rule weren't necessary, then there would be at least one pair of propositions of the form ⌈X is running⌉ and ⌈X is moving⌉ such that we may not infer the latter (e.g., "Socrates is moving") from the former (e.g., "Socrates is running"), in which case the proposition "If Socrates is running then Socrates is moving" would not be necessarily true. But from the non-necessity of the inference rule it would not follow that for *any* pair of propositions of the form ⌈X is running⌉ and ⌈X is moving⌉ we may not infer the latter from the former; if, *per impossibile*, the proposition "Socrates is moving" weren't inferable from the proposition "Socrates is running," the proposition "Plato is moving" might still be inferable from the proposition "Plato is running," so that the proposition "If Plato is running then Plato is moving" would still be necessarily true. Indeed, every proposition of the form ⌈If X is running then X is moving⌉ except for "If Socrates is running then Socrates is moving" could be necessarily true

27. As we noted in footnote 8, Bonaventure sometimes expresses an inference rule as a proposition (as in ibid., 82). We may either read him uncharitably as blurring the distinction between axioms and inference rules, or more charitably as gesturing toward the dependence of an inference rule's necessity on the necessary truth of related axioms.

as axioms, so that the inference rule in question is non-necessary. On this development of Bonaventure's position, the necessity of an inference rule depends on the necessary truth of all of a certain group of axioms, but not vice versa. Inference rules neither reduce to axioms nor logically follow from them, but a certain group of axioms all *need to be necessarily true* in order for a given inference rule to be necessary. The dependence of an inference rule's necessity on the necessary truth of all the relevant axioms is what dimly reflects the begetting of the Son by the Father in transcendent necessity. Furthermore, the dependence of a necessary conclusion's truth on the necessary truth of the axioms and the necessity of the inference rule(s) by which it is deduced from those axioms dimly reflects the procession of the Spirit from both the Father and the Son in transcendent necessity.

We have reached a pivotal point in our commentary on St. Bonaventure's treatise where we find ourselves evenly balanced between philosophy and theology. So far, Bonaventure's concerns have been primarily philosophical without excluding theology. Beginning in the next chapter, Bonaventure's emphasis will become increasingly theological without leaving philosophy behind entirely. We may regard the present chapter as a sort of frontier between two regions which are nonetheless parts of a single land. Now is especially a good time to pause for refreshing rest, relaxation, meditation, and prayer before we resume our study. I offer no discussion questions or suggestions for further reading, only the opportunity for a peaceful pause.

FIVE

God Confiding in Us

In his account of the soul's journey into God, Bonaventure is guided by his beliefs and his desire to find the truth. His beliefs provide him with some notion of what conclusions he should try to prove, and his desire spurs him to determine whether there are any good reasons for these conclusions. By the present stage of inquiry, Bonaventure takes himself to have discovered prima facie plausible philosophical proofs for at least some of his beliefs, including the existence of a transcendent First Principle, the existence of timeless ideas in the First Principle which also exist in our senses whenever we perceive external objects, and a threefold differentiation in the necessity of the First Principle reflected by the three modes of necessity occurring in the world. Bonaventure takes these proofs to be available to any rational investigator because they are based on premises which are potentially obvious to everyone and employ shared methods of valid reasoning from true premises to true conclusions.

However, there are other beliefs Bonaventure and many readers of this commentary hold in the absence of any purely rational proof; indeed, Christian orthodoxy teaches that the truth of such beliefs cannot be established on the basis of universally available reasons but can only be apprehended in some other manner. For example, Christians believe that God is a Trinity of Persons sharing a single divine essence; they also believe that the Son, who is the second Person of the Trinity, assumed human nature in Jesus Christ, who is equally God and man. Bonaventure is emphatic that belief in the God-man Jesus Christ is no mere afterthought but absolutely essential to completing the soul's journey:

> When one has fallen down he must lie there unless someone lend a helping hand for him to rise [an allusion to Ps 41:9 and Isa 24:20]. So our soul cannot rise completely from these things of sense to see itself and the Eternal Truth in itself unless Truth, assuming human nature in Christ, has become a ladder, restoring the first ladder that had been broken in Adam.
>
> Therefore, no matter how enlightened one may be by the light of natural and acquired knowledge, he cannot enter into himself *to delight* within himself *in the Lord* [Ps 37:4] unless Christ is his mediator, who says *I am the door. If anyone enters through me, he will be saved; and he will go in and out and will find pastures* [John 10:9].[1]

---

1. Bonaventure, *Soul's Journey into God*, 87–88.

The biblical references in this passage indicate that Bonaventure accepts both the brokenness of human nature and the need for Christ as mediator as true teachings that are found in sacred Scripture.

Some philosophers view the willingness to hold beliefs without having any proof of them as intellectually irresponsible. This attitude finds expression in the following remark from a recent philosophy book: "It seems to us that what there is no argument for, there is no reason to believe. And what there is no reason to believe, one *has* no reason to believe."[2] From the context of the remark, it becomes clear that by an "argument" the authors primarily have in mind what we described above as a prima facie plausible philosophical proof from universally available true premises to the intended conclusion via shared methods of valid reasoning. Presumably the notion of an acceptable argument here is understood broadly enough to encompass mathematical proofs as well as the non-deductive procedures of empirical justification characteristic of the natural sciences. The authors do not regard the mere fact that a belief is taught in Scripture as an acceptable argument for it. Since there is no acceptable argument for many beliefs Bonaventure and others hold on faith, it would seem to follow that there is no reason to hold those beliefs, and hence that Bonaventure and his co-religionists *have* no reason to hold them.

Notice that the attitude presented in the previous paragraph overlooks the teaching of Christian orthodoxy, according to which the truth of some beliefs cannot be established on the basis of universally available reasons—by an "accept-

2. Fodor and LePore, *Holism*, xviii.

able argument," if you will—but can only be apprehended in another manner. What is the basis for this teaching? Are there universally available, prima facie good reasons for it? More precisely, is there a universally available, prima facie good reason for thinking that there are no universally available, prima facie good reasons for or against at least some of the beliefs Bonaventure and others hold on faith, so that if they are indeed true their truth must be apprehended differently?

For the purposes of epistemological clarification, it will help to tell a parable. Once upon a time a man was hunting deep in the forest. As he was stalking a deer he came across an infant abandoned in a remote clearing. Taking pity on the child, the huntsman brought her to his hut. He decided to raise the child all by himself. For the next twenty years, the huntsman stayed with the girl in his rustic hut far from human habitation, caring for her as his own daughter, educating her, and teaching her how to survive by herself in the wilderness. The girl was never exposed to another human being. Eventually she grew up and the huntsman died, leaving her all alone in the woods. She decided to spend the rest of her life there. Years and years of her solitary existence passed until she was a very old woman. Far away in the village at the edge of the forest, the inhabitants heard rumors about the solitary woman who had spent well over eighty years in the wilderness, mostly by herself. They became extremely curious to learn how she had passed her time, what thoughts and activities occupied her days, what she was like as a person. The villagers wished to know something of the substance of her long life alone.

Let us now reflect philosophically upon our parable by considering the best way for the villagers to learn about the solitary woman. Suppose that they attempt to gather universally available reasons from which they may reach true and definite conclusions concerning her life. The reasons may include any empirically verifiable facts, and the methods of reaching conclusions include not only deductive inference but also any procedures of empirical justification characteristic of natural science. Despite these impressive epistemological resources, the villagers' chances of successfully deploying them to discover the substance of the solitary woman's life are extremely remote, if not impossible. The reason is that the character of her life alone is severely underdetermined by the totality of reasons and justificatory procedures available not only to the villagers but to any other rational investigator besides her. She may have passed most of her time composing poetry in her head, or hunting, or cultivating wildflowers, or weaving, or meditating on nature. Who knows? There are no experts to consult, for the solitary woman has never encountered another living human being. She has left no diary. Even if in their speculations the villagers somehow managed to hit upon an accurate description of the substance of her long life in the woods by herself, it would merely be a lucky guess. Such a description would not be justified on the basis of the paltry evidence available to them. Furthermore, not just the villagers but anyone who reflects on the foregoing scenario realizes the impossibility of justifying true and definite conclusions about the solitary woman's life on the basis of universally available reasons. That is, there is a universally available good reason for thinking that there are no universally available good reasons revealing the substance of her life.

How can the villagers learn anything about the solitary woman? The obvious way is for her to come forth and tell them about herself. She might describe her thoughts and activities during her many decades alone in the forest. She might show them samples of works she has created. In telling the villagers about herself she might reveal fundamental aspects of her character, such as her gentleness and kindheartedness. She might also display her attitude toward the villagers as one of compassion rather than indifference by bringing them gifts. She might even indicate the sort of relationship she desires to have with them as one of cooperation rather than enmity by offering to help them with various problems they face. The villagers can learn all of these things only through the solitary woman revealing herself to them. They cannot learn any of these things on the basis of reasons which are universally available independently of her self-revelation.

I suggest that for Bonaventure and others who hold on faith many of the same beliefs he does, God is like the solitary woman in our epistemological parable. God is a living being whose intrinsic existence and interior activities are radically apart from us. As such, the prospects of our inferring or otherwise justifying true and definite conclusions about God's life, character, and attitudes solely on the basis of universally available reasons are as remote as the chances of the villagers' learning about the solitary woman's life, character, and attitudes solely on the basis of similar reasons. Since this point can be grasped by anyone reflecting on the possibility of divine being who is radically apart from us in its very essence, there is a universally available good reason for thinking that there are no universally available good reasons justifying a number of true and definite conclusions about God. If there is a God then the only way for us to learn anything definite about His interior life, such as the eternal procession of the divine persons in the godhead; or about fundamental aspects of His character, such as His love and justice; or about His attitude toward us, such as His mercy and compassion; or about the sort of relationship He desires with us, such as abiding friendship, is for Him to tell us and show us by revealing Himself to us.

Why should we trust God concerning what He reveals to us about Himself? A similar question can be asked about the solitary woman: why should the villagers trust her concerning what she reveals to them about herself and the substance of her life in the forest? In the case of the solitary woman, plainly she is in a privileged position to report about her life because it is *her* life. If she comes forth from the forest and begins to tell the villagers about herself, they would determine whether or not to trust her based on her demeanor and the overall coherence of her story, not unlike how a jury gauges the reliability of a witness testifying on the stand. Parts of her story might be corroborated by acts she performs in their presence; for example, she might confirm her claim to have spent years thinking deeply about mathematics by quickly proving a difficult mathematical theorem the villagers have so far been unable to prove. Depending upon how God chooses to reveal Himself to us, some of these same factors might be relevant in establishing our trust; for example, if God reveals Himself by assuming human nature, the God-person's holy demeanor, effective teaching, and ability to perform miraculous good acts would certainly dispose witnesses to trust that individual's self-description.

Yet in whatever way God might choose to reveal Himself to us, Bonaventure has a more fundamental reason for trusting God concerning what He reveals to us about Himself.

From our discussion in chapter 2, remember that one conse-quence of Bonaventure's proof by exclusion for the existence of a transcendent First Principle is that the First Principle exhibits power, wisdom, and goodness in a way that includes without being limited to human wisdom, power, and good-ness. In particular, as the First Principle, God possesses moral goodness to an even greater degree than we do. Lying about one's life—interior or otherwise—or misrepresenting one's character, or concealing one's true attitude toward others is blatantly incompatible with the degree of moral goodness humans can possess, let alone with the even greater degree of moral goodness God possesses. Accordingly, if God exists and chooses to reveal Himself to us, then we have every rea-son to trust and no reason to doubt His self-revelation.

We have been pondering in somewhat abstract terms the possibility of truths about God which we can only know on the basis of divine self-revelation, in contrast with truths about God which we can establish on the basis of universally available reasons via shared methods of acceptable argument. It is now time to consider Bonaventure's description of the particular manner in which God reveals to us truths about Himself which we cannot come to know on the basis of purely rational proofs. Whereas the previous stage dealt with seeing God "through the mirror" of our mental powers of memory, intellect, and choice as vestiges, the present stage deals with seeing God "in the mirror" of the human soul as image. Bonaventure concentrates on our powers of intellect and choice, here treating memory as part of the intellect since concept retention is indispensable for thinking. He is inter-ested in how our exercising these powers might enable us to attain "intellectual illuminations" so that "our mind like the house of God is inhabited by divine wisdom."[3] Bonaventure isn't trying to *prove* that we can see God in the mirror of the human soul. For then he would have to prove that what we see about God there is true, which he can't because ex hypothesi there is no purely rational proof of the truths in question. Rather, Bonaventure's objective is to provide a coherent and genuinely informative conception of how God reveals Himself in the mirror of the human soul, given the Seraphic Doctor's prior belief in a God who chooses to reveal Himself to us. Even someone who doesn't share these religious beliefs can still inquire whether there is any such conception.

Bonaventure's account of how the human soul properly exercises its intellectual and volitional powers to become a mirror in which God can be seen is governed by three parameters. The first parameter is that such a soul has been reformed so as to literally *resemble* what is divine: "And so the image [the human soul] is reformed and made like the heavenly Jerusalem."[4] Unlike our sense organs, which themselves don't literally resemble God even when they are informed by divine ideas, the reformed soul with its intellectual and volitional powers is a special kind of image (*imago*) that is a likeness (*similitudo*) of God, or at least of divine order ("the heavenly Jerusalem"). Bonaventure says that our soul becomes a likeness of the divine once "our spirit is made hierarchical."[5] Specifically, he thinks the hierarchy of the reformed soul's habitual intellectual and volitional acts conforms to the hierarchy of angels and other divine realities.

3. Bonaventure, *Soul's Journey into God*, 93.
4. Ibid., 89.
5. Ibid., 90.

According to Bonaventure's second parameter, the reformed soul is directly aware of external spiritual realities:

> For in this stage, when the inner senses are restored to see the highest beauty, to hear the highest harmony, to smell the highest fragrance, to taste the highest sweetness, and to apprehend the highest delight, the soul is prepared for spiritual ecstasy through devotion, admiration, and exultation according to the three exclamations in the Canticle of Canticles.[6]

In the same section Bonaventure speaks of the soul recovering "its spiritual hearing and sight," "the spiritual sense of smell," and "its senses of taste and touch." He also claims that the reformed soul's direct awareness of external spiritual realities "is more a matter of affective experience than rational consideration."

Finally, the third parameter attributes the reforming of the soul, and thus the hierarchy of its intellectual and volitional acts, to the theological virtues of faith, hope, and charity operating in the soul: "The image of our soul, therefore, should be clothed with the three theological virtues, by which the soul is purified, illumined, and perfected."[7] Since Bonaventure maintains that these virtues can exist to varying degrees in different individuals—even those who are not undertaking the seven-stage spiritual journey he describes—his account of how the soul can become a likeness of God has broad repercussions for how God might reveal Himself to us and how we might respond.

6. Ibid., 89.
7. Ibid.

Can a coherent and informative conception of God's self-revelation in the mirror of the human soul be developed on the basis of these three parameters? A possible method is to begin by interpreting one parameter and then extending the interpretation to the other two. Let us apply this method by starting with the first parameter, according to which the reformed soul literally resembles what is divine because there is a hierarchy in the soul's intellectual and volitional acts conforming to divine hierarchies.

Bonaventure's notion of an order in the soul reflecting an external order suggests the influence of Plato. In the *Republic*, to discover what justice is in the individual Socrates and his interlocutors set out to determine what justice is in the city.[8] Eventually they arrive at the answer that the just city is one in which philosopher-monarchs command soldiers to rule workers. In the soul of the just individual there is a tripartite order corresponding to this tripartite order in the just city: the just individual is one whose wisdom commands her courage or fortitude to rule her passions. Similarly, Bonaventure writes,

> Our soul is also marked with nine levels when within it the following are arranged in orderly fashion: announcing, declaring, leading, ordering, strengthening, commanding, receiving, revealing, and anointing. These correspond level by level to the nine choirs of angels. In the human soul the first three of these levels pertain to human nature; the next three, to effort and the last three, to grace.[9]

8. See Plato, *Republic* II, 368.
9. Bonaventure, *Soul's Journey into God*, 90.

A well-ordered soul's intellect is illuminated by faith in God as the wisdom whereby He announces and declares Himself as a being supremely worthy of love. Faith then leads the soul to obey divine ordering and commanding so that the soul is strengthened against being "allured away by concupiscence."[10] These volitional acts are fortified by hope revealing the possibility of receiving in this life the sanctifying grace of charity as love of God above all other things for His own sake and of being anointed in heaven with everlasting charity through eternal union with Him. To the extent that different ecclesiastical bodies within "the Church militant"[11] on earth, different portions of sacred Scripture,[12] or even different kinds of angels perform these diverse functions, there is a hierarchy in these external realities conforming to the hierarchy within the reformed soul.[13]

By associating the hierarchy of the reformed soul's intellectual and volitional acts with properly knowing God, obey-

10. Ibid., 87.

11. Ibid., 89.

12. See ibid., 91.

13. For example, some angels may instruct us in divine matters, other angels may encourage our efforts and protect us from temptation, and yet others may inspire us to greater love of God by contemplating Him eternally. In the Church there are catechists who teach the faith, bishops who defend it from error, and religious who devote their lives to works of charity. And whereas Exod 20:1–17 and John 3:16–18 teach us about God's laws and His incarnation, respectively, Paul's letters contain many exhortations and warnings aimed at encouraging and protecting the Christian life, while the Song of Songs poetically portrays the mutual charity of God and His people. Bonaventure takes the idea of the hierarchy in the reformed soul conforming to the nine-fold angelic hierarchy from the mystical theology of Pseudo-Dionysius the Areopagite.

ing God with confidence of eventual success, and loving God, our interpretation of the first parameter makes some connection between this hierarchy and the theological virtues of faith, hope, and charity. Even so, it remains obscure exactly how these virtues exist or operate in the reformed soul. A more serious problem arises when we try to extend the interpretation to the second parameter, according to which the hierarchically ordered reformed soul has direct awareness of the corresponding divine hierarchies. We can appreciate the problem by going back to Plato's example of justice in the individual and justice in the city. Suppose that Elena is a perfectly just individual, in that her wisdom commands her courage to rule her passions. Suppose also that Paris is a perfectly just city, in that its philosopher-monarchs command its soldiers to rule its workers. Hence the hierarchy in Elena's soul conforms to the hierarchy in Paris. Yet obviously it doesn't follow that Elena is *directly aware* of Paris. She may never have heard of that city! For the same reason, from the fact that the hierarchy in a reformed soul conforms to angelic, ecclesiastical, and scriptural hierarchies, it doesn't follow that such a soul is directly aware of angels, the church, or sacred Scripture—let alone of God who creates and sustains these hierarchically ordered things.[14]

14. Echoing St. Bernard of Clairvaux, Bonaventure says that God dwells in the hierarchically ordered angels "and performs all their operations" (ibid., 90). Elsewhere he describes the angels as "receiving from the First Cause, God, an influx of power which, in turn, they distribute in their task of governing" the universe (2.2, 70). Perhaps Bonaventure would also say that God dwells in and performs all the operations of participants in ecclesiastical and scriptural hierarchies. However, even if this strong view of God's causal immanence is true it doesn't solve our problem. For suppose that the philosopher-monarchs,

Instead, let us start with the second parameter and try working our way to the other two. How can the reformed soul be directly aware of external spiritual realities? When Bonaventure speaks of spiritual *seeing, hearing, smelling, tasting*, and *touching*, he suggests that this direct awareness is like our sensory experiences of external objects. Yet as terms "spiritual" and "the inner senses"[15] indicate, Bonaventure has in mind not acts of sensing but acts of judging and choosing the soul performs by exercising its intrinsic intellectual and volitional powers. His basic idea is that there can be mental acts which, like sensory experiences, involve direct awareness of external things but, unlike such experiences, don't involve the use of sense organs. Bonaventure might observe that we do seem to have direct intellectual and volitional awareness of internal things: namely, our own sensory acts. For example, I may judge that my seeing an elm tree in glaring light is unpleasant and choose to terminate my act of seeing by shutting my eyes or turning away from the tree. In judging that my sensory act is unpleasant and choosing to terminate it, in some sense my soul is directly aware of my sensory act. Since immaterial information consisting of divine ideas exists in my sensory act, my soul is also directly aware of these external spiritual realities. Consequently, there is no reason in principle why my soul can't be directly aware of *other* external

---

soldiers, and workers of Paris have received an influx of causal power from the original builders which they then distribute in governing the city. It still wouldn't follow that Elena is directly aware either of Paris, of the influx of causal power from the original builders, or of the builders themselves. Later in this chapter we will return to the notion of a divine causal influx.

15. Ibid., 89.

spiritual realities, such as angels or even God Himself, in performing intellectual and volitional acts.

Unfortunately, it is difficult to see how this interpretation of Bonaventure's second parameter can be extended to his other two parameters. In the foregoing argument the soul need not literally resemble the divine ideas of which it is directly aware by having some hierarchical order it shares with them. In particular, there needn't be a hierarchy of the soul's intellectual and volitional acts instilled by faith as proper knowledge of God, hope as confidently obeying God, and charity as loving God for His own sake. But then the argument can be turned on its head: if the soul can be directly aware of divine ideas informing its sensory acts without the soul resembling the ideas—that is, without there being a hierarchy of the soul's intellectual and volitional acts that is brought about through the operation of faith, hope, and charity and conforming to some hierarchical order in the ideas—then there is no reason in principle why the soul can't be directly aware of *other* external spiritual realities, including angels and God Himself, without resembling these realities by sharing with them a hierarchy which, in the soul, is instilled by the operation of the theological virtues. Previously we could not get from hierarchy and the virtues to direct awareness; we now find ourselves unable to connect direct awareness with hierarchy and the virtues.

The last alternative is to start with the third parameter, according to which the soul is made hierarchical through the operation of faith, hope, and charity. Is there some way of understanding the operation of these virtues in the soul that explains how it is made hierarchical and also becomes directly

aware of external spiritual realities? Bonaventure does link
direct awareness with the efficacy of faith, hope, and charity:

> Filled with all these intellectual illuminations,
> our mind like the house of God is inhabited by
> divine Wisdom; it is made a daughter of God, His
> spouse and friend; it is made a member of Christ
> the Head, His sister and coheir; it is made a temple
> of the Holy Spirit, grounded on faith, built up by
> hope and dedicated to God by holiness of mind
> and body. All of this is accomplished by a most
> sincere love of Christ which *is poured forth in our*
> *hearts by the Holy Spirit who has been given to us*
> [Rom 5:5], without whom we cannot know the
> secret things of God.[16]

He then makes a provocative remark about *how* the theological virtues operate in the soul:

> No one can know *the things of man except the spirit*
> *of man which is in him; so no one knows the things*
> *of God except the spirit of God* [1 Cor 2:11].[17]

Expanding this ellipsis, we may say that no human being
properly knows, confidently hopes for, or loves God except
through the spirit of God which is in that human being.

Perhaps Bonaventure is saying that faith (supernatural
knowledge of God) and charity operate in a human soul when
God, who knows and loves Himself, dwells in that soul in the
person of the Holy Spirit. Although God doesn't *hope* to be
united with Himself eternally, since He already is, maybe the
indwelling of His self-knowledge and self-love in a human

16. Ibid., 93.
17. Ibid.

soul somehow instills in that soul the confident hope of its being eternally united with God in heaven. The trouble with this reading is that it makes faith and charity acts, not of a soul in which they operate, but of God who dwells in that soul. Yet if faith and charity exist in my soul then clearly I, not God, am the one who has faith and charity.

An earlier passage suggests a somewhat different reading. Bonaventure writes that "the governance of the universe is attributed to them [the angels], by their receiving from the First Cause, God, an influx of power which, in turn, they distribute in their task of governing, which has to do with the natural consistency of things."[18] God as First Cause creates all other beings and conserves them in their existence, including the angels. When the angels govern the universe, they do more than merely exist. Hence the influx of causal power they receive from God and then distribute in their task of governing is beyond the causality whereby God creates them and conserves them in their existence.[19] However, this additional influx of divine causality doesn't deprive the angels of *their* causality. Otherwise, the angels could not be said to "govern" or assist God in "governing" the universe; God alone would govern. Rather, God's causality works with the angels' causality to govern the universe. An analogy will help. Imagine that I use a stick to push a stone down the path. In pushing the stone with the stick, I don't directly cause the stone to move as I would if I pushed the stone with just my hand. Instead, I indirectly cause the stone to move by causing the stick to

18. Ibid., 70.

19. Traditional philosopher-theologians use the term "general concurrence" to designate the divine causal contribution that goes beyond creation and conservation.

cause the stone to move. Both my causality as the power to grip and manipulate natural objects like sticks and the stick's causality as the power to move appropriately-sized stones when properly manipulated are involved in producing the effect of pushing the stone down the path.[20] Similarly, perhaps Bonaventure takes the influx of power the angels receive from the First Cause to consist in God's causality working through the angels' causality to govern the rest of the universe.

What might the influx model of causality have to do with the operation of faith, hope, and charity in a reformed soul? For one thing, in cases where X causes Y to cause Z there is a hierarchy of causes, since the exercise of Y's causality is subordinate to X's exercise of its causality.[21] Thus if God causes a soul to cause its intellectual acts of faith (announcing, declaring, receiving) and its volitional acts of hope (ordering, strengthening, commanding) and of charity (receiving, revealing, and anointing), then the soul's causality in producing these acts is subordinated to God's causality so that there is a causal hierarchy in the soul. For another thing, just as sticks don't naturally go around pushing stones down paths but must be manipulated by a higher cause to do so, human souls don't naturally exercise their intellectual and volitional powers to perform acts of faith, hope, and charity but must

20. For more on causal powers and an account of what it is for something to have a particular property in terms of causal powers, see Shoemaker, "Causality and Properties."

21. In later Scholasticism, some causes in a given series (the stick pushing the stone displacing dust motes in its path, etc.) are said to be "essentially ordered" to another cause (my gripping and manipulating the stick). For more on essentially ordered causes and other kinds of essential order, see Scotus, *A Treatise on God as First Principle*, sections 1.3–1.16.

be animated by God to perform these acts. It might be argued that, comparable to how my manipulating the stick to push the stone down the path is a non-natural use of the stick's natural causal power, God's animating a soul to produce in it acts of faith, hope, and charity is a supernatural use of the soul's natural intellectual and volitional powers.

However, explaining the operation of faith, hope, and charity in terms of the influx model of causality isn't entirely satisfactory either. Applying this model to the soul's volitional acts which are associated with hope and charity is particularly problematic. Even if God implants in the soul not only faith as a supernatural knowledge of Him but also divine commands and exhortations, the soul must still obey these commands and exhortations in order to enjoy eternal union with God. Therein lies the rub, for the soul's acts of obedience must be *freely done*. Without attempting an analysis of free will here, we can observe that the stick caused by me to cause the stone to move does not in any sense act freely. Hence if the soul is caused by God to cause its acts of obedience in the same way the stick is caused by me to cause the stone to move, then in no sense does the soul act freely when it obeys divine commands and exhortations.

In our epistemological parable, the solitary woman comes forth to reveal to the villagers truths about herself which they cannot discover on their own: the substance of her life, fundamental aspects of her character and attitude toward the villagers, and the kind of relationship she desires to have with them. To reveal these truths she may do various things in their presence, but she also *speaks* to the villagers in order to get them to understand and to be her friends. She might speak to the villagers en masse, or conceivably she might speak to a single villager when he is all by himself. In either case, her speaking doesn't cause the desired effects in the way that my grasping and manipulating the stick causes it to move the stone. For example, if the solitary woman tells a lone villager Liam about herself with the purpose of getting him to be her friend, whether he becomes her friend isn't caused by her speech but is a result of his own free choice. Nonetheless, there is a hierarchy of acts since Liam's choosing depends on his understanding, which in turn depends on the solitary woman's speaking to Liam in order to get him to understand and to be her friend. If God reveals to us truths about Himself in a manner comparable to how the solitary woman reveals to the villagers truths about herself, then the possibility emerges of a speech-act model rather than a causal-influx model of the operation of faith, hope, and charity in a reformed soul. What the speech-act model requires is a plausible explication of how God might speak, either to individuals collectively or to an individual "one-on-one" in the interior of his/her soul.

A framework for developing such an explication can be extracted from the Oxford philosopher J. L. Austin's description of speech-acts.[22] Austin considers cases of speaking in which someone makes a promise, issues a command, makes an assertion, and so forth. In each case the speaker performs what Austin calls the *locutionary act* of uttering or writing particular words (e.g., "I promise to be home by noon," "Get me a saw," "Bonaventure was deeply influenced by Plato and Augustine"). Secondly, there is the *illocutionary act* the speaker performs by uttering or writing the words in question (e.g., promising her husband to be home by noon,

22. The most detailed description is found in Austin, *How to Do Things with Words.*

commanding his co-worker to get him a saw, asserting to the students in the class that Bonaventure was deeply influenced by Plato and Augustine). Thirdly, the speaker may perform some intentional or unintentional *perlocutionary act* by performing the illocutionary act in question (e.g., reassuring her husband, irritating his co-worker, getting the students to understand Bonaventure's intellectual debt to Plato and Augustine). A number of philosophers, including H. P. Grice, Stephen Schiffer, John Searle, and others, have offered varying accounts of the different types of speech acts and the interrelations among them. For our purposes it is unnecessary to delve into these details. Instead, let us think about whether the basic distinctions Austin draws can be used to explicate how God might speak to us.

Since she is a human being like we are, typically the solitary woman utters with her lips and tongue or writes with her fingers words in some natural language when she speaks. However, she may also perform illocutionary and perlocutionary acts by performing other kinds of locutionary acts; for example, by sending smoke signals she may tell the villagers that an enemy is approaching in order to warn them of an impending attack. This observation is important because it suggests that God may perform illocutionary and perlocutionary acts by performing locutionary acts even though He is an immaterial spirit with no lips, tongue, or fingers.[23] For example, if anything causable by secondary causes is directly causable by God, then God can tell the villagers that an enemy is approaching in order to warn them

23. Of course, if God is incarnated in a particular human being, then as such He typically speaks by uttering or writing words like the rest of us.

of an impending attack by directly causing the smoke signals Himself. Or He might directly cause vocal sound waves that are words in a natural language, as at the Baptism of Jesus and later at his Transfiguration. Another example is provided by 1 Kings 19:12 where God speaks to the prophet Elijah not in the strong and heavy wind, the earthquake, or the fire He causes but in "a tiny whispering sound" or, in the translation of the King James Version, "a still small voice." By causing a gust of wind to hit her in the face from the north, God can command a pilgrim not to take the north fork in a road, thus frightening her and warning her of wolves there. Or by causing a shaft of intense sunlight to fall on a certain spot, God may promise the pilgrim that the destination of her journey isn't far ahead in order to put her at ease. Many are the ways in which God might perform illocutionary and perlocutionary acts by performing locutionary acts besides moving lips, tongue, or fingers.

The nine levels Bonaventure describes in the reformed soul can be interpreted as a series of hierarchically ordered acts. Some of these acts are divine, others are human. Some are speech acts, others intellectual or volitional acts. By performing some non-standard locutionary act, God performs the illocutionary act of announcing and declaring to the soul that He is a being supremely worthy of love for His own sake. He does so with the intention of getting the soul to acquire the requisite supernatural knowledge of Himself. Since the reformed soul is led to acquire the requisite knowledge, God also performs the intentional perlocutionary act of leading the soul to have faith. God's perlocutionary act depends not just on the locutionary and illocutionary acts God performs but also on the intellectual act of receptive understanding the soul performs. The soul's intellectual act of faith *depends* on God's illocutionary act of announcing and declaring Himself to the soul, for without the illocutionary act the soul cannot arrive at faith in a loving God on the basis of universally available good reasons. Yet God's illocutionary act of declaring and announcing Himself need not *cause* the soul's intellectual act of faith. God simply announces and declares Himself to the soul in the foreknowledge that the soul will respond with its act of receptive understanding.

Furthermore, by performing other non-standard locutionary acts God performs the illocutionary act of issuing certain commands to the soul with the intention of persuading the soul to obey them. God also performs illocutionary acts of promising the soul that it will be eternally united with Him in heaven. God's intention in making this promise is to strengthen the soul so that it ultimately perseveres in hopeful obedience when confronted with challenges during its time on earth. Since the reformed soul obeys God's commands (including His commands concerning how to restore sanctity if it be lost through sin) and ultimately perseveres in obedience, God also performs the intentional perlocutionary acts of persuading the soul to obey Him and of strengthening the soul in ultimate perseverance. These divine perlocutionary acts depend not only on the corresponding divine illocutionary acts but also on the soul's volitional acts of obeying and persevering. God's illocutionary acts of commanding and promising don't cause the soul's volitional acts of obeying and persevering; as a free agent, the soul causes them. However, the soul's volitional acts essentially depend on God's illocutionary acts, in that the former are impossible without the latter.

In heaven God reveals to the soul a permanent vision of His essence. It is unclear whether this revelation should be construed as an intentional perlocutionary act God performs by performing some heavenly illocutionary act, or perhaps in another fashion. Upon receiving the beatific vision and fully loving what it beholds, the blessed soul (along with its resurrected and glorified body) is anointed with everlasting charity. In the beatified soul there are no more acts of faith or hope; there are only the soul's everlasting acts of vision and charity. The anointing of a blessed soul depends on God, His act of revealing His essence to the soul in heaven, and the soul's everlasting acts of vision and charity. These everlasting acts of the soul in heaven depend on the soul's earlier intellectual acts of faith and volitional acts of obeying and persevering in response to God's illocutionary acts of declaring, commanding, and promising during the soul's time on earth, without the everlasting acts being caused by the earlier acts in a manner that precludes free will.

In clarifying the operation of faith, hope, and charity in the reformed soul, the speech-act model satisfies the first parameter by explaining how a soul that has been made hierarchical conforms to divine hierarchy. It isn't so much that the order in the soul's intellectual and volitional acts mirrors a wholly external divine order, but rather that the order in the soul's acts is part of a broader divine order. For the soul's intellectual acts of faith and vision and its volitional acts of obedience and everlasting charity essentially depend on God's declarations, commands, promises, and revelations. As we have seen, Bonaventure holds that these latter divine acts may be further mediated by divinely ordained realities—including different kinds of angels, different ecclesiastical bodies in the church, and different portions of sacred Scripture. Thus through the requisite intellectual and volitional acts, the reformed soul becomes fully integrated into a single divine order pervading both the temporal "Church militant" and the eternal "heavenly Jerusalem."

Does the speech-act model also explain how a reformed soul is directly aware of external spiritual realities like angels and God Himself, as the first parameter requires? Up to now we have taken for granted an intuitive yet vague understanding of the distinction between direct and indirect awareness. The haziness of this distinction renders the prospect of a satisfactory answer remote, since we can't determine whether direct awareness of external spiritual realities is possible if we don't really know what direct awareness is as opposed to indirect awareness. The contrast between our coming to know truths about an agent on the basis of his/her speech acts to us and our coming to know truths about the same agent on the basis of universally available good reasons we can gather supplies a useful context for endowing the distinction between direct and indirect awareness with substantive content. If the villagers could somehow arrive at definite truths about the solitary woman's life in the woods from universally available good reasons, they would have indirect awareness or knowledge of her, as opposed to the direct awareness or knowledge they have of her if she comes forth from the forest and tells them about her life. Bonaventure's proof by exclusion for the existence of a First Principle on the basis of the trans-categorical characteristics of material things provides us with indirect awareness or knowledge of God "through a mirror," as opposed to the direct awareness or knowledge we have of Him when He or His representatives address us and we then choose how to respond. Hence in the foregoing context the difference between indirect and direct awareness of an agent boils down to the difference between learning whatever we can about the agent on the basis of widely available evidence and entering into an intimate, lifelong relationship with the agent initiated by his/her confiding in us. By performing non-standard locutionary acts, God and angels can perform various illocutionary and perlocutionary acts that draw us into an intimate relationship with these spiritual beings. Therefore, on the speech-act model there is no reason in principle why we cannot be directly aware of such external spiritual realities.

We conclude this chapter with two important caveats.

First, the context we have extracted from Bonaventure's work for understanding the distinction between direct and indirect awareness or knowledge of external spiritual realities should not be taken to imply that there are two distinct disciplines: philosophy as knowledge of God on the basis of universally available good reasons, and theology as knowledge of God revealed to us through divine speech. This kind of intellectual dualism is foreign to Bonaventure, Aquinas, and their Scholastic contemporaries. Nowhere in *The Soul's Journey into God* does the Seraphic Doctor embrace a rigid architectonic of natural theology versus revealed theology; instead, as we have seen, there is a gradual shift from concerns which are primarily philosophical without excluding theology to concerns which are primarily theological without excluding philosophy. For his part, the Angelic Doctor (Aquinas) envisages a single sacred science containing truths revealed to us in Scripture and corroborated by reason, either by demonstration or the removal of apparent conceptual difficulties.[24] Theology for them is simply the totality of humanly knowable truths about God and an account of how we know them. Some of these truths we can know on the basis of universally available good reasons. Others of these truths we can know only on the basis of divine revelation. In terms of our epistemological parable, a biography of the solitary woman covering her entire life might includes truths about her time alone in the woods which are supported only by her own testimony and truths about her time with the villagers supported by widely available empirical evidence in the form of records, photographs, and recordings. Nonetheless, the solitary woman has only one biography.

The second caveat is that on the speech-act model God can speak to us in numerous ways. He may declare Himself to a lone contemplative in "a still small voice," a mystical vision, or inner words heard only in the depths of the contemplative's soul. He may also speak to many people, either through intermediaries or without them. God's declarations, commands, promises, and expressions of love to humanity may be recorded by writers of sacred Scripture, which Bonaventure says "deals principally with the works of reparation" and hence "treats mainly of faith, hope, and charity by which the soul is reformed, and most especially of charity."[25] Similarly, the solitary woman may choose to communicate truths about her life, character, and attitudes to the villagers in numerous ways: by speaking to them herself, by speaking to someone who then reports what she said more or less verbatim, by speaking to someone who records her speech and then pres-

24. See *Summa Theologiae* 1a q.1, especially a.3 and a.8.
25. Bonaventure, *Soul's Journey into God*, 91.

ents it to the villagers, by delegating someone to speak for her in his own words, or even by appropriating something said or written by someone she hasn't delegated and then using it to communicate with the villagers.[26] In any of the multifarious modes God may choose to speak to us, through the reforming of our souls resulting in our deeper participation in divine order we come to have direct awareness or knowledge of Him and other external spiritual realities that is totally unlike the indirect awareness or knowledge we can attain through universally available good reasons.

DISCUSSION QUESTIONS

(1) Does God declare Himself to *every* human soul, so that some souls never enjoy beatitude because they don't respond by performing the intellectual or volitional acts also required for beatitude? Or does God only declare Himself to *some* human souls but not others?

(2) If the proper intellectual and volitional acts of a reformed soul leading to beatitude essentially depend on God's initial illocutionary act of declaring Himself to the soul, and if God declares Himself to some souls but not others, then is God responsible for the fact that the souls to whom He doesn't declare and announce Himself never enjoy beatitude?

26. For a fascinating description of the many modes of discourse whereby one may speak, see Wolterstorff, *Divine Discourse*, chapter 3. My remarks about the speech-act model are deeply influenced by Wolterstorff's sophisticated account of divine speech.

(3) Does God declare and announce Himself to non-Christians as a being supremely worthy of love for His own sake with the intention of reforming their souls, and if so then how?

SIX

God as Pure Being

Bonaventure avers that we can see God either "through the mirror" of His vestiges or "in the mirror" of His images. The vestiges through which we can see God consist of external material things and our internal mental powers. In each case, there is a proof by exclusion from features of things in the universe (the trans-categorical characteristics of material objects; the necessity of axioms, inference rules, and conclusions comprehended by human minds) to the existence of something not in the universe (a First Principle that is supremely powerful, wise, and good; a transcendent necessity in which there is a threefold differentiation). The images in which we can see God consist of our sensory activities and our intellectual and volitional powers reformed by grace. In the case of our sensory activities, there is a proof by constructive elimination from the ideas existing in our senses whenever we perceive external objects and also existing eternally in the divine mind. In the case of our mental powers reformed by grace, by performing the requisite intellectual and volitional acts in response to divine illocutionary acts the reformed soul is integrated more deeply into a pervasive divine order, culminating in the soul's eternal beatitude.

At the fifth stage of the soul's journey into God, Bonaventure tells us that

> We can contemplate God not only outside us and within us but also above us: outside through His vestiges, within through His image and above us through the light which shines above our minds, which is the light of Eternal Truth, since "our mind itself is formed immediately by Truth itself." [Vulgate Ps 4:7][1]

What is it to contemplate God "above us through the light of Eternal Truth"?

At 5.2, 95 Bonaventure explains that we can think about or contemplate God in different ways based on which primary name of God (*primum nomen Dei*) we have in mind. One way "fixes the gaze primarily and principally on Being itself, saying that God's primary name is *He who is*" (*qui est*). This primary name of God isn't the English phrase "He who is" or its Latin translation but the concept of being itself, or pure being, that they both express. In the same passage Bonaventure identifies a second way of thinking about God based on "the name of goodness" (*bonitatis*). The primary name of God here is the concept of goodness itself, or superexcellent goodness (*superexcellentissimam bonitatem*).[2] Let us designate

---

1. Bonaventure, *Soul's Journey into God*, 94.
2. See ibid., 105.

these primary names or concepts of God as *pure being* and *superexcellent goodness*, respectively. As the current stage "is concerned with the essential attributes of God,"[3] it seeks to determine what, if anything, can be known about God based on our understanding of *pure being*; whereas the next stage will discern what, if anything, can be known about God based on our understanding of *superexcellent goodness*.[4]

A concept is instantiated when there actually is something to which it applies. The concept *dog* is instantiated because there are dogs; the concept *unicorn* is not because there are no unicorns. Normally our understanding of a concept isn't sufficient for knowing whether it is instantiated. For example, I can understand the concept *Tasmanian devil* in that I know what it is for something to count as a Tasmanian devil yet not know whether there really are any Tasmanian devils. Does the same point hold for the concept *pure being*? Bonaventure's answer is no: "being itself is so certain in itself that it cannot be thought not to be."[5] In other words, once we fully understand *pure being* we see that this concept not only is but indeed must be instantiated. Bonaventure thus appears to endorse a version of St. Anselm's celebrated "ontological argument" utilizing the concept *pure being* rather than *that than which none greater can be conceived*.[6]

3. Ibid., 94.

4. Since Bonaventure's ontology doesn't include concepts as distinct entities, primary names are ultimately divine ideas capable of informing our intellects, though presumably not our senses. At this stage of inquiry Bonaventure may treat these two divine ideas as if they were concepts or notions so as not to prejudge whether there is a divine being that possesses them.

5. Ibid., 96.

6. See Anselm, *Major Works*, 82–122 for the classic presentation,

Before examining the details of Bonaventure's argument, let's step back and ask what purpose this argument is supposed to serve in the soul's journey into God. Typically the ontological argument is viewed as a freestanding, philosophical proof from our understanding of a particular concept like *pure being* or *that than which none greater can be conceived* to the concept's instantiation. Yet if Bonaventure intends his argument as a freestanding proof, it seems odd for him to present such a proof in the later and predominately theological portion of his treatise. A better place would be at an earlier and more philosophical stage, perhaps alongside the proof by exclusion for the existence of a transcendent First Principle. On the other hand, Bonaventure's argument does look like an attempt to prove God's existence on the basis of something universally available to all rational investigators regardless of whether they share the Christian faith—in this case, a concept they can all understand. And the argument certainly does not look like an attempt to provide a coherent and informative conception of some religious belief for which there is no universally available rational basis. Admittedly these observations aren't decisive. Bonaventure may present the proof at a relatively late stage because he thinks it is more excellent than other proofs, given that it proceeds from a pure concept rather than from any empirical observations and thus in an intuitive sense is closer to God as supremely excellent. Or perhaps upon closer inspection the "proof" turns out to be more theological than at first blush. We need to keep an open mind about the nature of Bonaventure's argument

elaboration, and defense of this argument. See Oppy, section 2 for a useful taxonomy of different versions of the ontological argument; Oppy prefers to speak of "ontological arguments."

until we have a better grasp of it. At the end of this chapter we shall return to the question of how the argument fits into the overall course of the soul's journey.

Bonaventure says that thinking about God in terms of *pure being* "is concerned with the essential attributes of God."[7] Does he mean that *pure being* itself is an essential attribute or a perfection of God? We might then take Bonaventure to be arguing along the following lines: By definition God is perfect. Hence God must possess all perfections. One of these perfections is *pure being*. Therefore, God must possess *pure being*, which is to say God must really exist. Notoriously, the inference from the premise that by definition God must possess the perfection of *pure being* to the conclusion that God must really exist is no more valid than the inference from the premise that by definition a perfect skyscraper must possess the perfection of actual being to the conclusion that a perfect skyscraper must really exist. However, as we shall see later in his chapter Bonaventure makes clear that by "the essential attributes of God" he means traditional divine attributes or perfections such as being uncaused, eternal, simple, unchangeable or impassible, infinite, and all-powerful. He does not list *pure being* as a perfection or essential attribute; instead, he treats the foregoing attributes as essential properties of what he thinks can be proven to instantiate the concept *pure being*: i.e., pure and divine being itself, or God. In Bonaventure's scheme, the instantiation of *pure being* is the subject of divine perfections, not one of them. Since Bonaventure's argument differs from the definitional argument sketched above, it isn't vulnerable to the same objection.

7. Bonaventure, *Soul's Journey into God*, 94.

The key to appreciating the kind of argument Bonaventure is presenting is a principle he enunciates in the following passage:

> For pure being occurs only in full flight from nonbeing, just as nothing is in full flight from being. Therefore, just as absolute nothing has nothing of being or its attributes, so contrariwise being itself has nothing of nonbeing either in act or potency, either in objective truth or in our estimation.[8]

Pure being contains no nonbeing, such as *capable of not existing*, either in its conceptual content or in our overall estimation of *pure being*. Otherwise the concept would not be *pure being* but some other concept *almost-but-not-completely-pure-being*. Accordingly, if something instantiates the concept *pure being* it contains no ontological nonbeing. Otherwise the entity in question would not instantiate *pure being* but some other concept. These points merely clarify what Bonaventure means by the term "pure being." I will call the conjunctive principle that *pure being* has nothing to do with nonbeing conceptually or in our overall estimation of it and that anything instantiating *pure being* has nothing to do with nonbeing ontologically *the Plenum Principle*.

Bonaventure's argument proceeds in two parts. First, he argues that *pure being* is instantiated. Second, he argues that what instantiates *pure being* is divine being: i.e., God. Using the Plenum Principle, let us reconstruct Bonaventure's reasoning in each part.

Part 1: If it is possible for *pure being* to be instantiated, then either (A) *pure being* is instantiated but could be not instantiated; or (B) *pure being* is not instantiated but could be instantiated; or (C) *pure being* is instantiated and it is not the case that it could be not instantiated—i.e., *pure being* must be instantiated.[9] Suppose that (A) is the case. Then *pure being* is instantiated by something X that possesses the potentiality not to exist. But by the Plenum Principle X doesn't instantiate *pure being* because X has something to do with ontological nonbeing, in that X possesses the potentiality not to exist even though it does exist. X may instantiate some other concept, but X doesn't instantiate *pure being* after all. Thus option (A) is rejected. Suppose next that (B) is the case. Then the following scenario is possible: *pure being* is instantiated by something Y that could exist but possesses the potentiality not to exist (since in fact Y doesn't exist). But by the Plenum Principle this scenario is not possible because in possessing the potential not to exist Y has something to do with ontological nonbeing and so does not instantiate *pure being* after all. Thus option (B) is rejected as well. Since (A), (B), and (C) are logically exhaustive options given the possibility for *pure being* to be instantiated, the only option left is (C). Hence if it is possible for *pure being* to be instantiated then *pure being* is instantiated by something Z that not only exists but indeed does not possess the potentiality not to exist, in which case Z must exist. Certainly it is possible for *pure being* to be instantiated since there is nothing intrinsically contradictory about the concept *pure being* that renders it incapable of being instantiated. Therefore, *pure being* is instantiated.[10]

9. The possibility for *pure being* to be instantiated is incompatible with the case in which *pure being* is not instantiated and could not be instantiated.

10. So reconstructed, Bonaventure's argument is an example of what

Part 2: There are only three possible kinds of being: non-divine particular being, analogous being, and divine particular being or God. Non-divine particular being consists in the individuality of such entities as stones, flowers, rivers, wolves, humans, planets, stars, and angels. Each of these entities has something to do with ontological nonbeing, since each of them possesses the potentiality not to exist and so is contingent.[11] As Bonaventure remarks, non-divine particular being is limited "because mixed with potency" for nonbeing.[12] By the Plenum Principle, it follows that no entity having non-divine particular being instantiates *pure being*. Analogous being consists in the accidental, generic, and specific properties of particular entities, both non-divine and divine, such as being red, being an animal, and being rational.[13] Bonaventure

---

Oppy calls a *modal* ontological argument. For a recent modal ontological argument, see Plantinga, *Nature of Necessity*. I avoid talk of "possible worlds" as foreign to Bonaventure, who prefers to link potentiality with nonbeing; for example, "It [what instantiates *pure being*] will appear to you as having no potentiality since every potential being [e.g., X and Y] has in some way something of nonbeing" (*Soul's Journey into God*, 97).

11. What about numbers, which if they exist are entities having particular being yet presumably lacking the potentiality for nonbeing? From our discussion in chapter 3 we know that Bonaventure regards numbers and any other necessarily existing mathematical entities as eternal ideas included within divine being.

12. Ibid., 96.

13. I am interpreting Bonaventure's use of "analogous being" (*esse analogum*) along the lines of the "analogy of inequality" described in Cajetan, *Analogy of Names*, 11–14. Cajetan takes specific, generic, and other properties to exhibit the analogy of inequality because different entities participate in the same property unequally: e.g., a human being is more perfectly an animal than a slug is, and the stars are more perfectly bodies than the earth is. Cajetan holds that the analogy of inequality is a lesser form of analogy than the analogy of proportionality he analyzes

claims that analogous being "has only a minimum of actuality because it has only a minimum of being,"[14] and so has something to do with ontological nonbeing. Presumably his reason is that since any accidental, generic, or specific property applies to some beings but not to other beings, beyond any analogous being there is always more being relative to which the analogous being in question has nonbeing. So again, by the Plenum Principle it follows that no analogous being instantiates *pure being*. The only kind of being left is divine particular being, which possesses no potentiality not to exist and beyond whose being there is no more being.[15] Therefore, *pure being* is instantiated by divine particular being, or God.

Having reconstructed Bonaventure's argument, let us now evaluate it. The argument raises many questions, not all of which we shall take up here. Instead, we will focus on a central objection to the reasoning in each part.

A crucial premise of the reasoning in part 1 is that it is possible for *pure being* to be instantiated. This premise was motivated with the observation that there is nothing intrinsically contradictory about the concept *pure being* that prevents its instantiation, in the way that there is something intrinsically contradictory about the concept *simultaneously square and not square* that prevents its instantiation. However, a

---

later (see ibid., 24–29 and *passim*). I am not necessarily attributing to Bonaventure the position, associated with Aquinas and Cajetan, that properties like *wisdom* as applied to God and creatures are themselves analogous rather than univocal or equivocal.

14. Bonaventure, *Soul's Journey into God*, 96.

15. To anticipate a bit, since divine particular being is simple yet also possesses a number of properties, these properties taken together are somehow the same as divine particular being. See the discussion question at the end of this chapter.

concept need not be intrinsically contradictory to be incapable of instantiation. For example, supposing that primary color concepts are primitive, the concept *simultaneously red all over and blue all* over cannot be instantiated even though its conceptual content is not explicitly contradictory. Or to take another example, there is nothing intrinsically contradictory about the concept *perpetual motion machine*; yet this concept cannot be instantiated because a perpetual motion machine is impossible. Similarly, it might be objected that for all we know the concept *pure being*—like these concepts—is incapable of instantiation even though its conceptual content isn't intrinsically contradictory. But then the crucial premise of the reasoning in part 1 is unjustified.

Bonaventure might reply that while for all we know *pure being* is incapable of instantiation even though it isn't intrinsically contradictory, it is also true that for all we know the concept is capable of instantiation. We just don't know. The problem with this reply is that the reasoning at part 1 becomes inconclusive because we don't know whether the crucial premise is true, in which case it should be neither asserted nor denied. But Bonaventure needs to assert the premise in order to make his argument.

A more interesting reply for Bonaventure to make deploys the epistemological rather than the metaphysical side of the Plenum Principle, according to which *pure being* itself contains no nonbeing either conceptually or in our overall estimation of it, where the latter includes not only our basic understanding or grasp of the concept but also anything that is potentially part of our total epistemic stance toward it. Let F be any concept that for all we know is incapable of instantiation even though F isn't intrinsically contradictory. To say that "for all we know" F is incapable of instantiation is to say that we currently do *not* know that F is capable of instantiation, in which case there is something of nonbeing in our overall estimation of F because out total epistemic stance includes our *not currently knowing* that F is capable of instantiation. But then by the epistemological side of the Plenum Principle F is not the concept *pure being* but some other concept. All the objection shows is that a concept like F which for all we know is incapable of instantiation isn't the concept *pure being*, not that the reasoning in part 1 is unsound or inconclusive.

The trouble with this reply is that it leaves us uncertain whether there really is any such concept as *pure being*. By construing "our overall estimation" in a suitably broad sense, Bonaventure can always deny that any concept F which is not intrinsically contradictory yet for all we know incapable of instantiation is the concept *pure being*, on the ground that there is something of nonbeing in our overall estimation of F but there cannot be anything of nonbeing in our overall estimation of *pure being*. Even by Bonaventure's lights it would seem impossible for there to be any such concept as *pure being*. After presenting his argument he muses, "Strange, then, is the blindness of the intellect, which does not consider that which it sees first and without which it can know nothing."[16] It is strange indeed. For if we can fail to consider *pure being* as that which we see first and without which we can know nothing else, then even once we eventually come to understand *pure being* properly there is something of nonbeing in our total epistemic stance toward the concept and hence in our overall estimation of it. The result is a contradiction: the con-

16. Ibid., 96.

cept we eventually come to understand both is *pure being* (by hypothesis) and is not *pure being* (because there is something of nonbeing in our overall estimation of it). Consequently, there can be no such concept as *pure being*.[17]

At least one other reply is open to Bonaventure. Immediately after the passage presenting the Plenum Principle he continues:

> Since nonbeing is the privation of being, it does not come into our understanding except through being; but being does not come to us through something else because everything which is understood is understood as nonbeing or being in potency or being in act.[18]

Conceptually, our understanding of nonbeing presupposes that we have some contrasting idea of being. Even nothing is only understood as the total absence of being. As we saw in chapter 4, from this conceptual dependence it doesn't follow that our idea of being corresponds to anything in reality. But Bonaventure can be read as asserting the stronger claim that nonbeing also depends ontologically ("in objective truth") on being. I will call the principle that nonbeing depends both conceptually and ontologically on being *the Non-Nullity Principle*.

Using the Non-Nullity Principle, Bonaventure may argue that even if there is some nonbeing in our overall estimation of *pure being*, nevertheless this concept must be instantiated. For suppose it is possible for *pure being* not to be

17. In chapter 8 we shall use this paradox to illuminate an aspect of Bonaventure's mystical theology.

18. Ibid.

instantiated, either because *pure being* is incapable of instantiation or because *pure being* is capable of instantiation and capable of non-instantiation (though not simultaneously). Since everything else that exists might not exist, there could then be a state of total nothingness in which there is no being whatsoever, pure or impure. By the Non-Nullity Principle, the nonbeing in a state of total nothingness depends ontologically on some actual being in that state. Consequently, the state in question isn't a state of total nothingness after all, for it includes some actual being on which the remaining nonbeing depends ontologically, as does any other state we might consider that includes a degree of nonbeing. Since the possibility for *pure being* not to be instantiated implies that there could be a state of total nothingness, and since there cannot be a state of total nothingness, there is no possibility for *pure being* not to be instantiated. Therefore, *pure being* must be instantiated.

The gist of this reply is the application of the Non-Nullity Principle to establish that the nonbeing in a state of total nothingness depends ontologically on some actual being in that state. Why? A state of total nothingness might be like the limiting situation we described in chapter 3, so that even though there is nothing it is possible for there to be something (e.g., a universe of material things) and this possibility itself is either necessary or not necessary. But a state of total nothingness might instead be such that not only is it the case that there is nothing, there cannot be anything at all and this necessity itself is either necessary or not necessary. In each of these cases, nonbeing—*there is nothing*—is exactly the same; by definition nonbeing lacks any positive features, and hence lacks any positive features it has in one of these cases but not the others. Thus nonbeing is metaphysically compatible with different modal circumstances. Since the nonbeing in a state of total nothingness cannot obtain without a definite set of modal circumstances also obtaining, other than nonbeing there is some being in virtue of which that definite set of modal circumstances obtains in a state of total nothingness.[19] But then it really isn't a state of total nothingness since it includes some being. Moreover, since this being is independent of nonbeing, it is pure being. Much more can be said about these issues.[20] Perhaps enough has been said to show that the objection raised against the first part of Bonaventure's argument is not decisive, since the idea that *pure being* isn't instantiated faces serious difficulties.

Turning now to part 2 of Bonaventure's argument, we saw that the Plenum Principle is indispensable for explaining why the instantiation of *pure being* is neither non-divine particular being nor analogous being but divine particular being or God. The Plenum Principle continues to play a central role later in the chapter, where Bonaventure argues that God has the traditional divine attributes of being uncaused, eternal, simple, wholly actual, unchangeable or impassible, infinite, and unique. Bonaventure's basic strategy is to argue that if divine being lacked any of these attributes then divine being

19. Might there be a state of total nothingness in which it is neither possible nor not possible for there to be something? Bonaventure may then be expected to ask what distinguishes this state of total nothingness from a state of total nothingness like the limiting situation in which it is possible for there to be something and a state of total nothingness in which it is not possible for there to be anything if in each case there is only absolute nonbeing and no positive being.

20. For more discussion, see Dillard, *Heidegger and Philosophical Atheology*, 89–101.

would have something to do with ontological nonbeing, so that contrary to what has already been proven divine being wouldn't instantiate *pure being*. For example, if divine being lacked the property of being uncaused then either divine being would be caused by something else, in which case divine being would possess the potentiality *not* to exist, or else divine being would pop into existence without any cause and so would *not* always exist. Either way, divine being would have something to do with ontological nonbeing. If divine being weren't eternal then either it would have a beginning or an end and so again would *not* always exist. If divine being weren't utterly simple then it would have component parts each one of which it is *not*. If divine being weren't entirely actual or if divine being could change, then it would possess the potential to be something it is *not*.[21] If divine being weren't infinite then it would be limited in some way and so there would some being beyond it which it is *not*.[22] And if divine being weren't unique then there would be more than one divine being so that each of these beings would *not* include the being of the others.[23] In each case, divine being

21. See especially Bonaventure, *Soul's Journey into God*, 97 for an account of these attributes.

22. See especially ibid., 99.

23. In ibid., 97–98 Bonaventure sketches a "superlative" argument for the uniqueness of divine being: since divine being exists by necessity, is uncaused, eternal, simple, maximally actual, and unlimited so that nothing can be added to it, divine being is most perfect. And since a superlative predication (e.g., "best," "most perfect") applies to one thing only, there is only one divine being. An objector might wonder why there can't be two beings which are equally necessary, uncaused, simple, maximally actual, and unlimited so that neither is "most perfect" but both are "tied for top honors," so to speak. A better argument for the uniqueness of divine being is that the being of one of these two beings

would have something to do with ontological nonbeing—an impossibility, given that divine being instantiates *pure being*. Bonaventure concludes that divine being possesses the attributes traditionally ascribed to it.

As we reflect on Bonaventure's liberal application of the Plenum Principle, a worry begins to take shape. Divine particular being is not the same as non-divine particular being or analogous being; God is not His creatures or any accidental, generic, or specific property. It is then unclear why the Plenum Principle cannot be used to prove that God qua divine particular being doesn't instantiate *pure being* after all. For since God is not His creatures, there is some being beyond or independent of God—i.e., the being of creatures and their properties—that God is not. Hence God has something to do with ontological nonbeing. But then, by the Plenum Principle God qua divine particular being doesn't instantiate *pure being*.

Bonaventure confronts the problem.[24] He admits that divine being is such that "nothing can be thought beyond it better, nobler or more worthy, hence nothing greater." In this respect divine being is unlike the being of Gaunilo's perfect island "than which nothing greater can be conceived," since by definition an island—even a perfect one—must be limited to exclude the being of the surrounding water.[25] Nevertheless, Bonaventure thinks there is a way for divine being to be all-

---

would still be limited to exclude that of the other being, so that the two beings wouldn't be truly unlimited. But then the extra "superlative" step that a being with all the aforementioned attributes is "most perfect" isn't needed.

24. See ibid., 97–100.
25. See Anselm, *Major Works*, 105–10.

inclusive and thus to instantiate *pure being* while maintaining a sufficiently sharp ontological distinction between God and creatures:

> It [divine being] is, therefore, all-inclusive not as the essence of all things but as the supremely excellent and most universal and most sufficient cause of all essences, whose power is supremely infinite and multiple in its efficacy because it is supremely unified in its essence.[26]

Divine being is also said to be "the universal principle of all multiplicity; hence it is the universal efficient, exemplary, and final cause of all things as 'the cause of being, the basis of understanding and the order of living' [a reference to Augustine, *The City of God*, VIII, 4]."[27] Bonaventure's idea is that God is the total cause of the actual being of any creature. By creating a creature God causes it to be actual rather than merely possible. God also conserves the creature in actual being during its existence and concurs with the creature's actual exercise of its powers. Every intelligible feature of the creature exemplifies an idea in the divine intellect, including the final cause or ultimate purpose of the creature's actual being. Since each and every aspect of any creature's actual being derives from some aspect of divine particular being, God's being virtually includes the being of each and every creature while remaining ontologically distinct from it. As Bonaventure puts it, divine particular being "is, therefore, totally within all things and

---

26. Bonaventure, *Soul's Journey into God*, 100.
27. Ibid., 99.

totally outside them . . . within all things, but not enclosed; outside all things, but not excluded."[28]

A doubt remains. As the total cause of every creature's actual being, need divine being resemble anything like the God of Christian orthodoxy? Consider a Neoplatonically inspired conception of divinity, according to which God is something like the obtaining of the following disjunctive fact: either universe U_1 (our universe) actually exists, or universe U_2 actually exists, or universe U_3 actually exists, and so on, for infinitely many mutually distinct possible universes; yet one and only one of these universes actually exists (ours). Imagine that the disjunctive fact is somehow also aware of its own obtaining. The obtaining of this self-aware disjunctive fact just *is* the actual existence of our universe U_1; there aren't two separate facts, U_1's actual existence and the obtaining of the disjunctive fact. To say that the actual existence of some universe is the same as the obtaining of the self-aware disjunctive fact is to say that former is an *emanation* of the latter (=God). Thus divine being is the same as the actual being of its emanation (=U_1), though if some other universe had emanated then divine being would have been the actual being of that emanation. From the potentiality of divine being to be some other emanation, it doesn't follow that divine being has anything to do with nonbeing. Divine being is just the obtaining of the self-aware disjunctive fact. If some other universe had emanated rather than ours, the self-aware disjunctive fact would have obtained to no greater degree than it actually does.[29] However, because divine being just is the

28. Ibid., 100.

29. Compare: if Gore had been elected president in 2000, the disjunctive fact that either Bush was elected president in 2000 or Gore

obtaining of the self-aware disjunctive fact there must be some emanation if divine being isn't to collapse into nonbeing. There must be some emanation or other of divine being, yet without its being determined which emanation there is. We may suppose that the particular universe which emanates or "expresses" divine being is determined by the self-aware disjunctive fact's timeless choice, in the same way that on the orthodox Christian view whatever universe God creates ex nihilo is determined by His timeless choice.[30]

The moderate Neoplatonic view described in the previous paragraph identifies the actual universe as one possible emanation or expression of divine being among others. On a stricter Neoplatonic view, divine being not only must emanate some universe it must emanate the actual universe, though there are transcendent aspects of divine being beyond its emanation. God's being isn't "exhausted" by God's emanation any more than a flooding river is exhausted by the water overflowing its banks. In either case, there is a reasonable sense in which divine being is the total cause of every creature's actual being because divinity emanates these creatures whose being is included within its own being. But then Bonaventure's solution to the problem of how divine being is both ontologically distinct from creatures and, as the instantiation of *pure being*,

---

was elected president in 2000 would have obtained to no greater or lesser degree than it actually does given that Bush was elected president in 2000.

30. The difference is that on the orthodox view, not only which universe God creates but whether He creates any universe at all is determined by God's timeless choice, whereas on the Neoplatonically inspired view *which* universe God emanates is determined by God's timeless choice but *whether* God emanates some universe or other is not.

also has nothing to do with nonbeing leaves open a quasi-pantheistic understanding of God that is totally at odds with the traditional theism of Christian orthodoxy.[31]

At the beginning of the chapter we asked whether Bonaventure's argument based on the primary name *pure being* is intended as a freestanding philosophical proof for the existence of God. We now have good reason to doubt this atomistic reading, since taken by itself Bonaventure's argument appears to be compatible with a wholly non-orthodox conception of divine being. Yet recall that Bonaventure also designates *superexcellent goodness* as a primary name. He compares the contemplation of God "above us" in terms of the primary names *pure being* and *superexcellent goodness* with the two golden Cherubim standing over the ark with its gilded lid, or mercy seat, in the Holy of Holies, the inner sanctuary of the Jewish temple. The image here is that of two angelic perspectives upon a single divine reality.

Bonaventure proceeds to analogize the first primary name/Cherub with the Old Testament and the second primary name/Cherub with the New Testament:

> The first looks chiefly to the Old Testament, which proclaims most of all the unity of the divine essence. Hence Moses was told *I am who I am* [Exod 3:14]. The second method looks to the New Testament which determines the plurality of

31. Some independent corroboration for the seriousness of this criticism lies in the fact that pantheistic metaphysicians such as Spinoza also endorse a version of the ontological argument. See Spinoza, *Ethics*, 85–88 (culminating in Proposition 7).

> Persons by baptizing *in the name of the Father and*
> *of the Son and of the Holy Spirit* [Matt 29:19].[32]

As a Christian, Bonaventure believes that the Old Testament is not a self-sufficient account of divinity but must be completed by the gospel of Jesus Christ in the New Testament. By associating the first and second method with the Old and New Testaments, respectively, Bonaventure implies that his reasoning based on *pure being* is not a self-sufficient proof of divine reality but must be supplanted with the richer Trinitarian and Christological considerations in his next chapter. Thus we have powerful textual evidence for interpreting his "ontological argument" as part of a broader philosophical and theological strategy. To understand this strategy, we must take our study to the next level of the soul's ascent.

DISCUSSION QUESTION

Suppose that both God and creatures possess the triple property of power, wisdom, and goodness. Since God is absolutely simple, God's triple property of power, wisdom, and goodness is the same as God, so that power, wisdom, and goodness in God are the same as each other. Yet since creatures can have great power without great wisdom or great goodness, great wisdom without great power or great goodness, or great goodness without great power or great wisdom, power, wisdom, and goodness in creatures are not the same as each other. Then how can God and creatures possess the same triple property of power, wisdom, and goodness?

---

32. Bonaventure, *Soul's Journey into God*, 95.

(a) Is there some distinction among power, wisdom, and goodness in God that is compatible with divine simplicity?

(b) Are power, wisdom, and goodness in creatures the different exercises of some single underlying creaturely power?

(c) If the power to discriminate colored shapes contains the sub-power to discriminate colors and the sub-power to discriminate shapes, where each of these sub-powers a can exist in something without the other sub-power, does it follow that the greater power to discriminate colored shapes has real "parts" or only that the lesser powers ways of participating in the greater power?

SEVEN

God as Superexcellent Goodness

The first way Bonaventure seeks to contemplate God "above us" utilizes the primary name or concept *pure being*. By itself that way is insufficient, since it is compatible with a quasi-pantheistic conception of the universe as an emanation of divine being, and so fails to reach the orthodox theistic conception of a transcendent God as the total cause of His ontologically distinct creation. However, as explained at the end of the previous chapter, we have reason to think that Bonaventure doesn't intend his reflections on *pure being* to be a self-standing proof but as part of a broader philosophical and theological strategy. There are two Cherubim over the mercy seat in the Holy of Holies, two ways of approaching one and the same divine reality. The second Cherub contemplates God by utilizing the primary name or concept *superexcellent goodness*. If the second Cherub is to the first as Bonaventure believes the New Testament is to the Old Testament, then metaphysical reflections on *pure being* must be completed with Trinitarian and Christological meditations on *superexcellent goodness*. Only then does our contemplation of the divine being "above us" reach God in His transcendent, ontologically distinct fullness.

Bonaventure opens his reflections on *superexcellent goodness* by observing how "the highest good . . . is such that it cannot rightly be thought not to be, since to be is in all ways better than not to be."[1] We might read Bonaventure as arguing that, like Plato's Form of the Good which is self-predicable and hence itself good, the concept *superexcellent goodness* is self-predicable and hence itself good to a superexcellent degree. Something is good to a superexcellent degree if and only if it is as good as it can possibly be. Since it is better for a concept to be instantiated than not to be instantiated *superexcellent goodness* is instantiated. But even granting premises that *superexcellent goodness* is self-predicable and that it is better for a concept to be instantiated than not, we only get the conclusion that *superexcellent goodness* instantiates itself and hence is good to a superexcellent degree. It is hard to attribute any philosophical or theological significance to this conclusion. The fact that *concept* instantiates itself because it is a concept is a triviality. Why is the fact that *superexcellent goodness* instantiates itself any less trivial? Perhaps there is something special about the latter concept that makes a difference. But Bonaventure doesn't explain what is so special about *superexcellent goodness*.

A more sympathetic reading of this opening argument situates it in the context of Bonaventure's earlier reflections

1. Bonaventure, *Soul's Journey into God*, 102.

on the instantiation of *pure being* by divine being. Since *superexcellent goodness* is a concept or property, it has some positive being. Suppose that divine being doesn't instantiate *superexcellent goodness*. Then there is some positive being beyond divine being that divine being is not, so that divine being has something to do with ontological nonbeing. By the Plenum Principle, the instantiation of *pure being* has nothing to do with nonbeing ontologically. Consequently, divine being doesn't instantiate *pure being*. Yet by the reasoning Bonaventure presents at stage five of the soul's ascent, we know that divine being *does* instantiate *pure being*. Therefore, the supposition that divine being doesn't instantiate *superexcellent goodness* is false: because divine being instantiates *pure being*, divine being instantiates *superexcellent goodness* as well.

We now come to the "masterstroke" of Bonaventure's meditation on *superexcellent goodness*. Bonaventure turns what looks like a liability for the Christian philosopher-theologian into an asset—three assets, in fact. The liability is the Neoplatonic metaphysics of emanation that is compatible with the wholly non-Christian views that the being of creatures isn't ontologically distinct from God's being and that God must emanate a universe. Rather than entirely repudiating the metaphysics of emanation, Bonaventure applies it to the good: "For good is said to be self-diffusive; therefore, the highest good must be most self-diffusive."[2] Since the diffusion, emanation, or expression of goodness is itself good, whatever is good is naturally inclined to diffuse, emanate, or express its goodness. Thus whatever is good to a superexcel-

2. Ibid., 103.

lent degree must diffuse its goodness as much as it possibly can; otherwise, it wouldn't be good to some degree it could be good, and so it wouldn't be good to a superexcellent degree. In particular, since divine being instantiating *pure being* also instantiates *superexcellent goodness*, divine being must diffuse its goodness as much as it possibly can. We may then ask whether creating the actual universe or perhaps some other possible universe constitutes a maximal diffusion of divine superexcellent goodness. Here Bonaventure draws a first asset from the apparent liability by answering with a resounding "No!": "For the diffusion in time in creation is no more than a center or point in relation to the immensity of the divine goodness."[3] No possible universe fully diffuses, expresses, or emanates the goodness of divine being, since there is always more to divine being than there is to the universe.[4]

We may next wonder whether *anything* constitutes a maximal diffusion of divine superexcellent goodness if diffusing a universe does not. Here Bonaventure answers with a resounding "Yes!" What maximally diffuses divine superexcellent goodness are "the emanations"[5] which are none other than the three divine Persons of the Holy Trinity:

> Therefore, unless there were eternally in the highest good a production which is actual and consub-

3. Ibid.

4. On the stricter Neoplatonic view described in the last chapter, clearly there is more divine being than there is to the universe it must emanate since there are transcendent aspects of divinity beyond its emanation. Even on the moderate Neoplatonic view we considered, at least *logically* there is more to divine being than there is to the actual universe since the latter is only one among infinitely many ways for the divine disjunctive fact to obtain.

5. Ibid., 102.

> stantial, and a hypostasis as noble as the producer,
> . . . and this is the Father, the Son, and the Holy
> Spirit—unless these were present, it would by no
> means be the highest good because it would not
> diffuse itself in the highest degree.[6]

Bonaventure now proceeds to draw a second asset from the apparent liability. As emanations of the divine being insofar as it possesses superexcellent goodness, the Persons are to divine being or the godhead as the actual universe is to divine being on a Neoplatonic conception. Thus there is no sharp ontological distinction between divine being and the being of its emanations. The idea of the universe as an emanation of divine being results in a heterodox pantheism or monism that blurs the difference between God and creatures. But the idea of the three Persons as emanations of divine being, Bonaventure thinks, results in the entirely orthodox Trinitarian thesis, according to which God and the Persons are "one in being" even though there are aspects of divinity beyond each divine Person. For example, no Person is "one in personhood" with another Person.[7]

A third asset Bonaventure draws from the apparent liability of the metaphysics of emanation is his complete break with the idea that God must emanate a universe. Since divine superexcellent goodness is maximally diffused in the three divine Persons *in extra* (i.e., internal to the divine essence), there is no necessity that God emanate anything good that is *ad extra* (i.e., external to the divine essence) in order for there

6. Ibid., 103.

7. In the next chapter we shall consider whether these and other differences within divinity nevertheless share fully in necessary divine being.

to be a maximal diffusion of divine superexcellent goodness. Specifically, the divine being instantiating both *pure being* and *superexcellent goodness* isn't necessitated to create *any* universe; and if it does create a universe *ad extra* then doing so adds no further goodness to the maximal diffusion of its goodness by the three divine Persons *in extra*.[8] Because the same divine being instantiates both *pure being* and *superexcellent goodness*, Bonaventure is able to tie up the thread left hanging by his reflections in the previous chapter: the pure and superexcellent divine being totally causes the ontologically distinct universe without being necessitated to do so.

With an appreciation for Bonaventure's masterful application of the Neoplatonic metaphysics of emanation to divine superexcellent goodness, let us next examine what threatens to be a lethal objection to it. Bonaventure maintains that divine being "is infinite."[9] Hence presumably divine being is infinitely good. In any case, there is no upper bound to goodness per se because no matter how good something is it can always be better. So for any number of emanations of divine superexcellent goodness it appears that there remain further emanations of divine superexcellent goodness. Therefore, it seems that a maximal diffusion of divine superexcellent goodness requires not a trinity but infinitely many divine Persons as emanations. However, this consequence is unacceptable for a theological reason and for a philosophical rea-

8. Later in this chapter we shall take up the question of whether the divine being instantiating *superexcellent goodness*, and thus whose superexcellent goodness is maximally diffused in the Trinitarian Persons *in extra*, can ever create a universe *ad extra* that is exceeded in being and goodness by the divine being.

9. Ibid., 99.

son. Theologically, there being an Infinity of divine Persons obviously conflicts with the Christian teaching that there is only a Trinity of divine Persons: Father, Son, and Holy Spirit. Philosophically, it is impossible for there to be infinitely many divine Persons as emanations. It might seem to be possible; after all, there are infinitely many natural numbers, so clearly it's possible for there to be infinitely many natural numbers. Why can't there be a maximal diffusion of divine superexcellent goodness by infinitely many divine emanations? The reason has to do with what is entailed by something's being an emanation. An emanation of X is a complete manifestation or a full expression of X. Hence emanation is like other forms of full expression, such as assertion. Suppose you had a thought that could only be asserted by a sentence containing infinitely many words. No matter how many words your partial sentence already contained, you would always have to add more words before closing the sentence with a period and asserting your thought by uttering the sentence. Clearly you could never close the sentence with a period because there would always be more words to add. But then you could never form a sentence and assert your thought by uttering it. Similarly, if there are always more divine Persons to emanate prior to there being a full expression of divine superexcellent goodness, then divine superexcellent goodness can never be fully expressed by emanating divine Persons.[10]

10. The need for infinitely many divine emanations prior to there being a full expression of divine superexcellent goodness is logically analogous to what is known as a *supertask* or *hypertask*: a task occurring within a finite amount of time that requires for its completion an infinite number of sub-tasks. See Salmon, *Zeno's Paradoxes* for more discussion. Strictly speaking, the emanating of infinitely many divine Persons by divine superexcellent goodness isn't a supertask because it doesn't occur

Let us see whether Bonaventure says anything that can be utilized to address this objection. He lists the six properties of supreme communicability, supreme consubstantiality, supreme configurability, supreme coequality, supreme coeternity, and supreme mutual intimacy shared by the godhead and its emanations.[11] These properties reflect the fact that the godhead and its emanations are one in being. Bonaventure continues:

> But when you contemplate these things, do not think that you comprehend the incomprehensible. For you still have something else to consider in these six properties which strongly leads our mind's eye to amazement and admiration. For here is supreme communicability with individuality of persons, supreme consubstantiality with plurality of hypostases, supreme configurability with distinct personality, supreme coequality with degree, supreme coeternity with emanation, supreme mutual intimacy with mission. Who would not be lifted up in admiration at the sight of such marvels?[12]

---

in time but in eternity. Yet it is logically similar in that for something to be (performing the main task, fully manifesting divine superexcellent goodness) something else impossible must be (performing infinitely many sub-tasks in a finite amount of time, "expressing" divinity through infinitely many emanations). Moreover, if an emanation fully expresses divinity comparable to how uttering a sentence asserts a thought, then the godhead cannot "express" infinitely many emanations in a manner analogous to how the grammatical rules for a language recursively express infinitely many grammatical sentences. For by uttering the grammatical rules, you do not thereby assert all the thoughts (even conflicting ones!) associated with those sentences.

11. See Bonaventure, *Soul's Journey into God*, 104.

12. Ibid., 104–5.

In short, along with the oneness in being of the godhead and its emanations, there is also the plurality of the emanations themselves. What is the principle of this plurality?

> Therefore, the one emanating and the one producing are distinguished by their properties and are one in essence. Since, then, they are distinguished by their properties they have personal properties and plurality of hypostases and emanation of origin and order, not of posteriority but of origin, and a sending forth, not involving a change of place but free inspiration by reason of the producer's authority which the sender has in relation to the one sent.[13]

The crux of this dense passage is that the relational properties of the divine emanations are what individuate these emanations from the godhead and from each other. We now need to unpack Bonaventure's idea and then determine whether it can be used to answer the above objection.

The relation between X and X's emanations isn't temporal but logical ("not of posteriority but of origin"): X's emanations don't come after X in time but logically depend on X. Since logical dependence is non-temporal, so is emanation, allowing divine emanations as relations of logical dependence to obtain in timeless eternity. All divine emanations ultimately emanate from the godhead. Bonaventure calls this common logical dependence of all emanations on the godhead "emanation of origin and order"; we shall designate it *primary emanating*. The godhead's superexcellent goodness implies that the godhead has the property of emanating if

13. Ibid., 105–6.

possible. Since each divine emanation is one in being with the godhead, each emanation also has the property of emanating if possible. We shall designate emanating of a divine emanation by some other divine emanation(s) *secondary emanating*. Let a divine relational property be a property something divine has only if it is primarily emanated and either secondarily emanates or is secondarily emanated by something else.[14] Since the godhead is not primarily emanated by anything, in itself it has no divine relational properties. However, because it is primarily emanated by the godhead, any divine emanation has some divine relational property. Therefore, the godhead is individuated from any divine emanation of it.

Divine emanations are individuated from each other by the different relational properties they have. For example, a divine emanation that is not secondarily emanated by any other divine emanation(s) and that secondarily emanates some other emanation(s) has the relational property Bonaventure designates as *originating*.[15] A divine emanation that is secondarily emanated by another divine emanation and that secondarily emanates some divine emanation(s) has the relational property Bonaventure designates as *producing*. And a divine emanation that is secondarily emanated by some divine emanation and that does not secondarily emanate any divine emanation(s) has the relational property Bonaventure

14. In this context I shall often speak simply of *relational* properties.

15. He also uses the term "the one emanating" (ibid., 105). To avoid confusion, I prefer the term "originating." Given Bonaventure's earlier use of "origin" to describe the relation of ultimate logical dependence of all divine emanations on the godhead, perhaps "begetting" would be a better choice. Yet as long as the difference between "originating" and "origin" is kept clearly in mind, I see no reason not to follow Bonaventure's usage here.

designates as *being a sending forth*. Bonaventure maintains that such relational properties are the sole basis for the individuation of divine emanations. Emanation E1 is identical with emanation E2 just in case there is no relational property E1 has that E2 lacks or vice versa.[16]

Given that divine emanations are individuated by their relational properties and that there are just the three aforementioned relational properties, it follows that at most there are only three divine emanations. For suppose that in addition to three emanations E1, E2, and E3 which have the relational properties of originating, producing, and being a sending forth, respectively, there is some further emanation En. Then either En possesses just one of these relational properties or En possesses some combination of them. If En possesses just one relational property—for example, if En is originating—then En possesses all and only the relational properties possessed by one of the other three emanations—for example, E1—and so it identical with it. If En possesses some combination of relational properties, then either it possesses all three of them or it possesses at most any two of them. But En can't possess all three relational properties, since then En would be both secondarily emanated and not secondarily emanated. For the same reason En can't possess any two relational properties where one of them is the property of originating. Neither can En possess the two personal properties of producing and being a sending forth, since then En would both secondarily emanate and not secondarily emanate. Hence En

16. Formally, where "x" and "y" are variables ranging over divine emanations and "P" is a variable ranging over divine relational properties, we have the following principle of individuation for divine emanations: $(x)(y)(P)[x = y \leftrightarrow (Px \leftrightarrow Py)]$.

can't possess some combination of the relational properties possessed by E1, E2, and E3. Therefore, there is no further emanation En in addition to these three. Bonaventure takes the relational properties of originating, producing, and being a sending forth to "put a halt" on emanating by limiting it to three divine emanations at most. Since the superexcellent goodness of the godhead and divine emanations one in being with it implies that the godhead and the divine emanations emanate if possible, there are exactly three divine emanations each possessing only one of the relational properties.

It might be asked why there are just the three divine relational properties of originating, producing, and being a sending forth. Consider the possible divine relational property *being a producing sending forth* which, like being a sending forth, is secondarily emanated but also which, like producing, secondarily emanates. Intuitively, a producing emanation could secondarily emanate another producing emanation, which could secondarily yet another producing emanation, and so on, ad infinitum. But then if whatever instantiates divine superexcellent goodness or is one in being with it must emanate if possible, there is no halt to emanating and divine superexcellent goodness isn't fully expressed after all. Or perhaps Bonaventure has overlooked additional divine relational properties not definable in terms of his original three which would generate further divine emanations/Persons.

I believe Bonaventure's answer to this question would be that what initially appears to be intuitively plausible is actually ontologically flawed. A divine emanation is producing just in case it is secondarily emanated and it secondarily emanates. For there to be a plurality of "producings" there must be some way of individuating ontologically distinct emanations which all share the relational property of being secondarily emanated and secondarily emanating. Yet according to Bonaventure, possibly influenced here by his Platonic inheritance, divine emanations are individuated solely on the basis of relational properties taken as primitive and thus as existing apart from anything possessing them. If we had some independent purchase on what it is for quasi-particulars to exist within the godhead—perhaps along the lines of Scotus's *supposita* as "existences" to which the divine essence is communicated but which themselves cannot be communicated—then we could identify divine emanations/Persons with such *supposita* and make sense out of different emanations/Persons sharing the same relational property of producing.[17] It also seems that we could make sense of an Infinity of divine Persons possessing any one of the relational properties: there could be infinitely many *supposita* possessing the property of originating, or of producing, or of being a sending forth. For this very reason, Bonaventure might reject on theological grounds any conception of divine emanations as quasi-particulars, instead individuating emanations in terms of primitive relational properties. As for the possibility of additional divine relational properties not definable in terms of the original three, Bonaventure may observe that the burden is on the objector to specify precisely what these additional properties are.

Two worries remain. First, the divine emanations are one in being with the godhead and thus participate fully in

17. For more on Scotus's notion of *supposita* and its role in his Trinitarian thought, see Cross, "Duns Scotus on Divine Substance and the Trinity." I describe *supposita* as "quasi-particulars" because these "existences" to which the divine essence is communicated can neither be particulars nor principles of particularity like Scotist *haecceities* without implying that there are Gods sharing the same divine essence.

divine being. Since divine being is infinite in the sense of un-limited, it follows that each of the three divine emanations is also infinite in this sense. We saw why there cannot be infinitely many divine emanations, but our development of Bonaventure's position leaves it unclear why each divine ema-nation is infinite. Second, even if originating, producing, and being a sending forth are primitive relational properties, what philosophical reason is there to think that they are *personal* properties? From all that has been said so far, originating, producing, and being a sending forth might be no more per-sonal than sprouting, growing, and fruiting. Let us address these worries in order.

In chapter 4 we considered how Bonaventure's view that we can see God "through the mirror" of our own mental powers can be developed into a prima facie plausible proof by exclusion for the existence of a transcendent necessity in which there is a threefold differentiation dimly reflected by the three modes of necessity occurring in our manifold dis-cursive practices. These three modes of necessity are those of necessary axioms, necessary inference rules, and necessary conclusions inferred from the axioms via the inference rules. Given Bonaventure's broad understanding of these notions, there is no reason in principle why there cannot be infinitely many axioms, infinitely many inference rules, and infinitely many conclusions. For example, the total set of axioms might include: "If Socrates is running then Socrates is moving," "If Plato is running then Plato is moving," and so on for infi-nitely many possible human beings.[18] Even if there aren't infi-

18. From our modern perspective we might express all these axioms with the universally quantified statement "For any x, if x is human and x is running then x is moving" that has infinitely many instances.

nitely many inference rules, each inference rule is schematic for infinitely many applications; applications of the rule "A proposition of the form ⌈if Q then P⌉ may be inferred from a proposition of the form P" include "'If Xanthippe is alive then if Socrates is running then Socrates is moving' may be inferred from 'If Socrates is running then Socrates is moving,'" "'If Xanthippe is alive then if Plato is running then Plato is moving' may be inferred from 'If Plato is running then Plato is moving,'" and so forth, through infinitely many such applications. But from the infinitely many axioms and the infinitely many applications of this inference rules there follow infinitely many conclusions: "If Xanthippe is alive then if Socrates is running then Socrates is moving," "If Xanthippe is alive then if Plato is running then Plato is moving," and so forth. It is open to Bonaventure to construe the infinitely many axioms, infinitely many inference rule applications, and infinitely many conclusions as reflecting, respectively, the infinity of the Father as originating emanation, the infinity of the Son as producing emanation, and the infinity of the Spirit as being a sending forth emanation. Divine emanations are finite because there can only be three of them. Yet they are also intrinsically infinite—as is the divine being with which they are commensurate—in a manner only dimly reflected by the infinities associated with the three modes of necessity occurring in our discursive practices.

What philosophical reason is there to think that the relational properties of originating, producing, and being a sending forth are properties of *persons*, let alone divine ones?

Bonaventure has no such notion of quantification available to him; even so, there is a sense in which the universal quantification is "infinite" in that its quantifier ranges over infinitely many objects.

The question assumes that there must be a purely philosophical explanation of why these properties are personal. Here it is important not to lose sight of our methodological observation at the beginning of chapter 4. If there is such an explanation, then unless there is some mistake in Bonaventure's reasoning we have overlooked, a purely philosophical proof exists not only for the conclusion that *pure being* and *superexcellent goodness* are instantiated by divine being but for divine being's existing as a Trinity of Persons. The doctrine of the Trinity would thus be demonstrable solely on the basis of a proof available to all rational investigators independently of faith—a consequence incompatible with the Christian understanding of the doctrine as something that can only be revealed supernaturally. It is the primarily theological matters we explored in chapter 5 which may now prove to be more pertinent: according to Bonaventure, is there any supernatural reason to think that originating, producing, and being a sending forth are personal properties?

Bonaventure writes:

> For the Cherubim who faced each other also signify this. The fact that they faced each other *with their faces turned toward the Mercy Seat* [Exod 25:20], is not without a mystical meaning, so that what Our Lord said in John might be verified: *This is eternal life, that they may know you, the only true God and Jesus Christ, whom you have sent* [John 17:3]. For we should wonder not only at the essential and personal properties of God in themselves but also in comparison with the super-wonderful union of God and man in the unity of the Person Jesus Christ.[19]

19. Bonaventure, *Soul's Journey into God*, 106.

Bonaventure links our wondering contemplation of the personal properties of God with our encountering the God-man Jesus Christ whom God has *sent*. Perhaps we human beings cannot grasp why originating, producing, and being a sending forth are personal properties except through the revelation of God in Jesus. Let us develop this idea by turning to key passages in the Gospel of John, beginning with the one Bonaventure cites.

John 17 in its entirety reads:

> When Jesus had said this [an answer to the disciples' questions about his departure from the world], he raised his eyes and said, "Father, the hour has come. Give glory to your son, so that your son may glorify you, just as you gave him authority over all people, so that he may give eternal life to all you gave him. Now this is eternal life, that they should know you, the only true God, and the one whom you sent, Jesus Christ. I glorified you on earth by accomplishing the work that you gave me to do. Now glorify me, Father, with you, with the glory that I had with you before the world began" (John 17:1–5).[20]

In this passage Jesus says that he is the son sent into the world to accomplish work he was given. A son is a person. A person isn't sent to accomplish work by wind, oceans, flowers, or animals but only by another person or persons. Jesus identifies the Father as the person who sent him to accomplish the work the Father gave him to do, and he describes himself as sharing glory with the Father before the beginning

20. All biblical passages quoted in my own text are from The New American Bible.

of the world into which the Father sent him. If we take Jesus to be performing illocutionary acts of speaking initially to the disciples and subsequently to us in order to perform the intentional perlocutionary act of revealing certain information about himself that we cannot otherwise know, then so far we have learned the following: before the beginning of the world there were two Persons sharing glory, the Father and his Son, Jesus Christ, whom the Father sent into the world to accomplish work the Father gave him.

Earlier, Jesus had promised the disciples another kind of sending:

> I have told you this while I am with you. The Advocate, the holy Spirit that the Father will send in my name—he will teach you everything and remind you of all that I told you (John 14:25–26).

In addition to the Son sent by the Father into the world, then, there is also the Spirit sent by the Father in the Son's name to teach the disciples and remind them of what Jesus told them. Since only a person or persons are sent to teach and remind, the Spirit sent by the Father in the name of the Son is also a person. Jesus later elaborates on the sending of the Spirit: "But I tell you the truth, it is better for you that I go. For if I do not go, the Advocate will not come to you. But if I go, I will send him to you" (John 16:7). Not just the Father but also the Son Jesus Christ sends the Spirit. Except in atypical cases not applicable here (as when a deceased person leaves a letter to a living person sending her to execute some task), a person sent by other persons coexists with them before being sent. So the Spirit coexisted with the Father and the Son before the beginning of the world. The Spirit is also designated as "holy," placing it on a par with the Father and the Son. Again, if we take Jesus to be speaking in order to reveal information that is not otherwise accessible to the disciples and us, we now learn that before the beginning of the world there were three holy and hence divine Persons: the Father, the Son, and the Spirit. The Father sends the Son into the world to accomplish the work the Father gave him; and both the Father and the Son send the Spirit to teach and remind.

On the basis of what has been revealed so far, we have also learned that the sending of the Son by the Father and the sending of the Spirit by the Father and the Son aren't non-personal relational properties like sprouting, growing, and fruiting but personal activities. Moreover, these different types of personal sending are ordered in a particular way. Nowhere is the Father said to be sent by anyone, so there is no personal sending of the Father. The Son is said to be sent by the Father, so there is a personal sending of the Son that depends only on a personal sending by the Father.[21] The Spirit is said to be sent by both the Father and the Son, so there is a personal sending of the Spirit that depends both on a personal sending by the Father and a personal sending by the Son. Since the Spirit does not come until the Son leaves the world into which he was sent by the Father, the personal sending of the Spirit also depends on the personal sending of the Son, which in turn depends on a personal sending by the

21. Person X sending person Y and person Y being sent by person X may be regarded as a single reality including two relational aspects or orientations, in the way that a single spatial reality such as the road between Athens and Thebes includes two directions: from Athens to Thebes and from Thebes to Athens. Aquinas develops this idea in *Summa Theologiae* 1a, q.28, a.4.

Father.[22] Finally, nowhere is the Spirit said to send anyone, so there is no personal sending by the Spirit.

If the three divine Persons coexisted before the beginning of the world, then they are Persons independently of any of the personal activities of sending or being sent which occur either in the world or after the Son leaves it. The Father is a father per se, independently of sending the Son into the world and of his and the Son sending the Spirit into the world; the Son is a son per se, independently of being sent into the world by the Father and of his and the Father's sending the Spirit into the world; and the Spirit is a spirit per se, independently of being sent into the world by the Father and the Son. Yet up to this point, Jesus speaks only about acts of personal sending or being sent occurring in the world or after he leaves it. Apparently his words tell us nothing about the activities of these Persons before the beginning of the world. Or do they?

In John 14:6–7, Jesus proclaims, "I am the way and the truth and the life. No one comes to the Father except through me. *If you know me, then you will also know my Father. From now on you do know him and have seen him*" (emphasis added). Jesus proclaims himself to be the way to the Father—not "the Father in relation to the world" but "the Father," period. Jesus also says that "a son cannot do anything on his own, but only what he sees his father doing; for what he does, the son will do also" (John 5:19). As such, what Jesus tells us

22. On one interpretation, the Father's sending of the Spirit consists in the Father's sending the Son who then sends the Spirit once the Son has left the world. On another interpretation, the Father's sending of the Spirit is an additional sending by the Father such that the sending of the Spirit depends on both this additional sending by the Father and the sending by the Son. The second interpretation is probably a more natural reading of the passages from John's gospel.

about himself in these passages isn't an isolated description of his activities on earth and after he leaves it but provides knowledge of the Son per se, including the Son's "doings" with regard to the other divine Persons coexisting with him before the beginning of the world. Thus while the Father is a father independently of sending the Son into the world and of his and the Son's sending the Spirit into the world, he is not a father independently of sending the coexisting Son and the coexisting Spirit before the world's beginning. And while the Son is a son independently of being sent by the Father into the world and of his and the Father's sending the Spirit into world after the Son leaves it, he is not a son independently of being sent by the coexisting Father and of his and the Father's sending the coexisting Spirit before the world's beginning. Finally, while the Spirit is a spirit independently of being sent by the Father and Son into the world, he is not a spirit independently of being sent by both the coexisting Father and the coexisting Son before the world's beginning. Since every personal sending of any divine Person depends on a personal sending by the Father, the latter sending is an *originating*. Since the personal sending of the Spirit depends on the personal sending by the Son, the latter sending is a *producing*.[23] Finally, since there is a personal sending of the Spirit but no personal sending by it, the latter is *being a sending forth*.

23. Since the personal sending of the Spirit also depends on a personal sending by the Father, the latter sending is also productive. But because this personal sending by the Father depends on no other sending, whereas the personal sending by Son does, the personal sending of the Spirit by the Son may be more narrowly designated as a producing.

The purpose of our brief Scriptural exegesis is not to re-solve all the complex issues of Trinitarian theology, several of which we shall highlight at the end of this chapter. Rather, our purpose is to put flesh on the bones of the idea that we can-not possibly comprehend how the properties of originating, producing, and being a sending forth Bonaventure identifies with the divine emanations are personal properties apart from the revelation of Jesus Christ as the Son who is sent by the Father and who together with the Father sends the Spirit. The only grip we have on how these Persons are a Father, a Son, and a Spirit is through what Jesus tells us about their interrelations of sending and being sent into the world. So if these Persons are a Father, a Son, and a Spirit even before the beginning of the world, these same basic interrelations must obtain then as well. Without Jesus' revelation of himself and the other Persons through his speech to the disciples and us, no matter how brilliant someone is intellectually she will never grasp the personal character of originating, producing, and being a sending forth.

Bonaventure's Christocentric understanding of the Trinity has potentially far-reaching theological ramifications. The Seraphic Doctor describes an angel as "the intellectual and incorporeal substance which, by the very fact that it is so similar to God, enjoys simplicity of nature and individu-ality of whatever concerns its substance, whether common or individual."[24] In other words, angels are intellectual sub-stances possessing a native intelligence as close to God's as any creature's can be. Some angels, the Seraphim, devote their entire existence to intense love of the Holy Trinity;

24. Bonaventure, *Breviloquium*, 77–78.

other angels, the demons, turn away from the Trinity and are punished with everlasting damnation. In either case, on Bonaventure's view the angels comprehend the Trinitarian Persons as divine emanations individuated by the personal properties of originating, producing, and being a sending forth, so that even before the beginning of the world the angels grasp these properties as personal. Since this grasp is not an achievement of natural reason but requires the revelation of the Persons through Jesus Christ, it follows that even before the beginning of the world the God-man in whom is joined "the most perfect and immense with the lowly" is revealed to the angels.[25] Presumably angelic knowledge of the Trinity doesn't depend upon human sin. However, if the Incarnation depended on redeeming us from sin, then angelic knowledge of the Trinity would depend on human sin after all. Therefore, the existence of the God-man doesn't depend upon human sin either. Later thinkers in the Franciscan tradition such as Duns Scotus develop this idea into the so-called "Franciscan thesis" concerning the motive of the Incarnation, according to which the God-man's essential purpose is to glorify the tri-une God, a secondary purpose being his redemption of our fallen humanity.[26]

Bonaventure's Christocentrism also enables him to close a gap in his metaphysics of creation. The divine being whose superexcellent goodness is maximally diffused *in extra* in

25. Bonaventure, *Soul's Journey into God*, 107. It might be that despite their powerful intellects the angels cannot grasp even the logical *possibility* of a being who is both God and human apart from God's revealing to them through limited foreknowledge of the *actuality* of the Son's incarnation in Jesus Christ.

26. For more discussion, see Dean, *Primer on the Absolute Primacy of Christ* and Dillard, "A Minor Matter?"

the Trinitarian Persons isn't necessitated to create anything *ad extra*. It might be objected that in fact such a being is necessitated not to create anything *ad extra*! For whatever a being instantiating *superexcellent goodness* creates *ad extra* must perfectly reflect that being's superexcellent goodness. Yet apparently nothing *ad extra* can perfectly reflect the divine being's superexcellent goodness because nothing *ad extra* instantiates *superexcellent goodness*. Only God does. Bonaventure can reply that although neither the universe nor any ordinary creature in it instantiates *superexcellent goodness*, Jesus Christ does because he is literally God as well as literally human. Accordingly, any universe the divine being instantiating *superexcellent goodness* chooses to create must include the God-man. This conditional necessity is compatible with the non-necessity of God creating anything *ad extra*.

We shall round out the present chapter by highlighting some issues raised by the Trinitarian theology Bonaventure sketches in chapter 6 of *The Soul's Journey into God*. After noting that the highest good must be most self-diffusive, Bonaventure goes on to say that "the greatest self-diffusion cannot exist unless it is actual and intrinsic, substantial and hypostatic, *natural and voluntary, free and necessary.*"[27] We might read Bonaventure as arguing that the highest good must possess every good, so that since being free is a good and being necessary is a good the highest good must be both free and necessary. But even if being free is a good and being necessary is a good, it doesn't follow that both of these goods can coexist in the same being. Perhaps these two ways of being good are comparable to being exclusively red and being exclusively blue, both ways of being exclusively colored which

27. Bonaventure, *Soul's Journey into God*, 103, emphasis added.

nonetheless cannot coexist in the same object. Divine being is necessary being, so since the divine Persons emanated by the godhead all share divine being they too possess necessary being. For this reason, divine emanating cannot be free in any sense of "being free" that allows for the contingency of what is freely done. If there is a way of freely emanating that is compatible with the necessary being of what is emanated, Bonaventure doesn't elaborate on it.

Bonaventure's solution is to maintain the necessity of divine emanating and ascribe freedom—in a sense that allows for the contingency of what is freely done—to the godhead and the divine Persons *in toto*:

> From supreme goodness it is necessary that there be in the Persons . . . supreme mutual intimacy, by which one is necessarily in the other by supreme interpenetration *and one acts with the other in absolute lack of division of the substance, power and operation of the most blessed Trinity itself.*[28]

The divine being, which is the being of the divine emanations maximally diffused *in extra* in the three Persons, is necessary. Yet this same three-in-one divine being is free in a sense that allows for the contingency of what it does or refrains from doing *ad extra*. For example, the three-in-one divine being is free either to create or not to create a universe, to speak or not to speak to intelligent creatures at specific places and times, to grant or not to grant prayer requests, and so forth. The divine being's free acts *ad extra* are ipso facto voluntary acts *ad extra* of the emanated divine Persons; the divine being's natural acts *in extra* of emanating these Persons are not voluntary but necessary.

28. Ibid., 104, emphasis added.

A glitch remains. It has to do with the fact that some voluntary acts or operations are ascribed to different divine Persons. We have already encountered some examples in our exegesis of the passages from John. The Father, not the Son or the Spirit, sends the Son into the world to accomplish the work that the Father gave him. The Son, not the Father or the Spirit, leaves the world to return to the Father after accomplishing this work. The Father and the Son, not the Spirit, send the Spirit to teach and remind after the Son's return to the Father. To deal with this sort of difficulty, St. Thomas Aquinas proposes that although all three Persons share their operations, in particular cases an operation is appropriated to a specific Person.[29] So while the Father, the Son, and the Spirit all act in concert to perform the operation θ whereby the Son is sent into the world, θ is appropriated to the Father as a sending by him. A question about this proposal is what warrants the appropriation of any particular operation to a specific Person. What warrants the appropriation of θ to the Father? Part of the reason may be to avoid the infelicity of saying that the Son sent himself into the world. But then what reason is there to appropriate θ to the Father rather than to the Spirit, given that there is no infelicity in saying that the Spirit sent the Son into the world? To be sure, sacred Scripture clearly describes the Father and not the Spirit as sending the Son into the world. Yet it might be worried that Aquinas's proposal muddles this clear teaching by treating as unitary an

29. See *Summa Theologiae* 1a, q.39. a.7, where Aquinas argues that the essential attributes of intellect and will can be predicated of all three Persons by appropriation. Since voluntary operations are acts of will, these operations can also be predicated of all three Persons by appropriation.

operation that in some sense really is specific to the Father, not merely appropriated as such.[30]

An alternative proposal accepts Scripture as teaching that different Persons perform specific voluntary operations of the same divine will and then offers a picture to illustrate this teaching. In a State consisting of executive, legislative, and judicial branches, distinct acts by members of these branches are still acts of state. A ruling that declares a certain law to be unconstitutional is a specific act of the judicial branch, not of the executive or the legislative branch. Nevertheless, this same act is an act of the entire State. Other organizations exemplify this sort of specific-yet-corporate willing. Since specific-yet-corporate willing exists, clearly it is possible and was possible even when nothing existed yet. By the Non-Nullity Principle, this possibility must depend ontologically on some actual being that existed even when nothing else existed. A candidate for such a being is the godhead in which different Persons have at least the power to perform specific voluntary operations which nevertheless are all voluntary acts of the godhead.[31] The picture is only a picture, not a proof. It is properly viewed as one opening statement in the ongoing and fascinating discussion of various views concerning Trinitarian economy.

30. For a more sympathetic attitude toward the medieval doctrine of appropriation, see Cross, "Duns Scotus on Divine Substance and the Trinity," 199–201.

31. Before the beginning of the world and unknown to us, the Persons may even actually perform distinct voluntary operations of knowing, communicating, and loving vis-à-vis one another that are all acts of the godhead. These acts and the power to perform them are different from the godhead's necessary emanating of the Persons.

At times Bonaventure's enthusiasm gets the better of him, leading him to say things that sound decidedly unorthodox:

> But if you are the other Cherub contemplating the properties of the Persons, . . . look at the Mercy Seat and wonder that in Christ personal union exists with a trinity of substances and a duality of natures; that complete agreement exists with a plurality of wills.[32]

The Trinity of divine Persons cannot be a trinity of substances without there being three gods—which is tri-theism, not monotheism. Nor does each Person possess its own will, resulting in a plurality of wills within the godhead. There is only one divine will. What Bonaventure may be expressing with the rather misleading phrase "a trinity of substances" (*trinitate substantiarum*) is that the same necessary divine being or substance is shared fully and equally by all three Persons. His remark about "a plurality of wills" (*pluralitate voluntatem*) may describe not the godhead but the personal union including a duality of natures, one divine and one human, in the God-man. Since the divine will is part of the divine nature and a human will is part of any human nature, in the God-man there exists a plurality (duality) of wills, one divine and one human, which are in complete agreement. Because Bonaventure rejects the Nestorian heterodoxy that there is a duality of divine and human persons in the God-

32. Bonaventure, *Soul's Journey into God*, 108. Alternatively, the trinity of substances that Bonaventure attributes to the Christ's personal union may consist of God as the divine substance, Christ's human soul as an immaterial substance, and Christ's human body as a material substance. The former substance constitutes Christ's divine nature and the latter two substances constitute Christ's human nature.

man, he holds the God-man to be one divine person, the Son. The human nature that is assumed by the Son isn't human nature in general but one specific human nature like the singular humanity of Socrates ("Socrateity"). This assumed humanity cannot itself be a person as long as it is assumed, even though it possesses a human will and a human intellect. What is highly compressed in Bonaventure's exposition is developed in considerable and often conflicting detail by other Scholastic theologians.[33]

Bonaventure's primarily philosophical reflections on "the first Cherub" or *primum nomen* of *pure being* must be supplemented by his primarily theological meditations on "the second Cherub" or *primum nomen* of *superexcellent goodness*. Merely on the basis of the fact that it instantiates *pure being*, without an understanding of the Trinitarian Persons necessarily emanated by what also instantiates *superexcellent goodness* the divine being cannot be distinguished as the transcendent and total cause of an ontologically distinct creation, as opposed to the immanent and ontologically inclusive source of the universe. And without the revelation of the Father, the Son, and the Spirit by the God-man Jesus Christ, there is no understanding of the Trinitarian Persons as *persons*. Therefore, Bonaventure provides no purely philo-

---

33. Aquinas regards Christ's assumed human nature as individuated by what he calls *material signata* or "signate matter" (the spatiotemporal continuity of this flesh and these bones); Scotus regards the nature as individuated by a *haecceity* or primitive "thisness." Aquinas and Scotus also differ in their accounts of why the individualized human nature assumed by Christ is not a human person. For an interesting discussion of these issues, see Reichmann, "Aquinas, Scotus, and the Christological Mystery" and the references in his text to relevant works by Aquinas and Scotus.

sophical "ontological argument" for the existence of God understood in traditional theistic terms. Of course, there may be
some other purely philosophical proof for the desired conclusion, such as one or more of Aquinas's Five Ways, Scotus's
Causal Argument, or even Bonaventure's own proof by exclusion, which we examined in chapter 2. But for Bonaventure, a
grasp of what instantiates both *pure being* and *superexcellent
goodness* is impossible apart from what is revealed to us by
the words of the Word, Jesus Christ.

We have almost completed our study of Bonaventure's
treatise as a way into Scholastic philosophical theology. In
our final chapter we shall confront a fundamental perplexity
that emerges at the apex of the soul's journey into God. We
must try our best to discern whether it is a perplexity that
must collapse into irresolvable paradox and antinomy or, as
Bonaventure believes, a perplexity that may lead to spiritual
ecstasy.

Discussion Question

If there being infinitely many axioms, infinitely many inference rules, and infinitely many theorems dimly reflects the
infinity of the Father as originating emanation, the infinity of
the Son as producing emanation, and the infinity of the Spirit
as being a sending forth emanation—since the set of axioms,
the set of inference rules, and the set of theorems are disjoint
sets—does it follow that the Father, Son, and Spirit each *know*
things not known by the other two Persons? Or does it only
follow that the Persons are both *metaphysically* necessary and
infinite in different ways, with no consequences for what the
Persons know or how They know it?

EIGHT

Ecstatic Contemplation

The Plenum Principle we encountered at the fifth stage of the soul's journey has an epistemological side and a metaphysical one. Epistemologically, the Plenum Principle maintains that the *primum nomen* of *pure being* has nothing to do with non-being in our overall estimation of it. Thus if some concept *F* either includes negative conceptual content, such as *capable of not existing*, or if there is something negative in our total epistemic stance toward *F*, such as our not knowing whether *F* is capable or incapable of instantiation, then *F* is not the concept *pure being*. Metaphysically, the Plenum Principle claims that anything instantiating *pure being* has nothing to do with nonbeing ontologically. Hence if some being X is capable of not existing or has the potential of being something it is not then X does not instantiate *pure being*.

In chapter 6 we noticed that the epistemological side of the Plenum Principle engenders a paradox. There can be nothing negative in our total epistemic stance toward the concept *pure being*. But Bonaventure himself says that we fail to consider *pure being* as that which we can see first and foremost and without which we can know nothing else. Indeed, our analysis of Bonaventure's philosophical and theological case for thinking that *pure being* and *superexcellent goodness* both are instantiated by the divine being of Christian orthodoxy is a story of doubt, worry, and uncertainty at every turn. All of these intellectual qualms are surely deficits in our knowledge of *pure being*. Therefore, by the epistemological side of the Plenum Principle the concept Bonaventure takes to be *pure being* really isn't. There appears to be no such concept after all.

Yet, as Bonaventure himself might also say, appearances can be deceiving. Let us slow the story down and scrutinize the epistemological nonbeing that Bonaventure describes (i.e., our failure to consider what is first and foremost) and that we have experienced (i.e., our intellectual doubts, worries, and uncertainties arising in the course of evaluating Bonaventure's reasoning at the fifth and sixth stages of the soul's journey). If at any point something of nonbeing exists in our overall estimation towards the concept under consideration, the epistemological side of the Plenum Principle together with the assumption that we grasp *pure being* vaguely and imperfectly at that point implies a contradiction. If we grasp *pure being* vaguely and imperfectly at that point, then we still grasp *pure being* at that point. But if we grasp the concept under consideration "vaguely and imperfectly" at that point, then by the epistemological side of the Plenum Principle we do not grasp *pure being* at that point but some other concept. Consequently, we both grasp and do not grasp *pure being* at the point in question, which is a contradiction.

It is open to Bonaventure to avoid this contradiction by rejecting the assumption that we grasp *pure being* vaguely and imperfectly at any point during which our knowledge of the concept is deficient. On the contrary, he can reply that we don't grasp *pure being* at all then. Rather, we only grasp *pure being* fully and instantaneously at some point after we have studied his philosophical and theological reasoning at the fifth and sixth stages and come through all our intellectual doubts, worries, and uncertainties about it. For the Seraphic Doctor, there is no gap whatsoever between our full and instantaneous grasp of *pure being* and our recognition that *pure being* is instantiated by the divine, Trinitarian being that also instantiates *superexcellent goodness*. Prior to that point, we may have mistakenly thought we grasped *pure being*, albeit vaguely and imperfectly, but what we really grasped—if anything—were merely conceptual approximations to *pure being*, not *pure being* itself.[1]

Although Bonaventure doesn't explicitly characterize our cognition that *pure being* and *superexcellent goodness* are instantiated by the divine being as a sort of instantaneous grasp distinct from our non-instantaneous grasp of quotidian concepts like *fox* and their instantiations, the view I have attributed to him fits naturally with his analogy of *pure being*

---

1. Blocking the objection that there is still something negative in our total epistemic toward *pure being* (because we previously thought we grasped it when we really didn't) requires a slight modification of the epistemological side of the Plenum Principle: *pure being* has nothing to do with nonbeing in our overall estimation while we are grasping *pure being*. Once you've really got it you know all there is to know about it. It would seem that this knowledge must also remain, at least as a permanent disposition of the soul, even when one sleeps or suffers brain damage impairing normal cognitive functioning.

and *superexcellent goodness* to "the Cherubim who faced each other . . . *with their faces turned toward the Mercy Seat.*"[2] The first Cherub contemplates "God's essential attributes."[3] The second Cherub contemplates "the properties of the Persons."[4] Both Cherubim gaze upon the Mercy Seat Bonaventure associates with the God-man Jesus Christ, who focuses their joint contemplation into a unitary angelic cognition of the Trinitarian God. No negative conceptual content or epistemic deficits are described before, during, or after this cognition. No angelic doubts, worries, or uncertainties are mentioned. Of a human mind undergoing this same cognition, Bonaventure says that "It reaches the perfection of its illuminations on the sixth stage."[5] A perfect illumination is all-at-once and all-or-nothing, a "flash" like the overhead light switching on to illuminate the entire room and its contents perfectly and instantaneously. Once perfection of illumination has been attained, there can be no diminution of it since it wouldn't be perfection if it could be diminished. In more contemporary terms, what constitutes the summit of human intellectual achievement isn't our mastery of general relativity or quantum mechanics or proof theory or advanced topology, but rather our instantaneous grasp that *pure being* and *superexcellent goodness* are instantiated by the divine being. It is the very best the human intellect can attain primarily on its own this side of the grave.[6] If not the letter, then at

2. Bonaventure, *Soul's Journey into God*, 106.

3. Ibid.

4. Ibid., 107.

5. Ibid., 109.

6. I say "primarily on its own " because, on Bonaventure's view, the human intellect's instantaneous grasp of the fact that *pure being* and

least the spirit of Bonaventure's remarks strongly suggests our reconstruction of his view.

It is the metaphysical side of the Plenum Principle, according to which whatever instantiates *pure being* has nothing to do with nonbeing ontologically, that threatens to wreak havoc at the end of the soul's journey. Put plainly, the Trinitarian divine being that Bonaventure takes to instantiate both *pure being* and *superexcellent goodness* appears to be shot through with ontological nonbeing! The divine essence is *not* the same as any of the three divine Persons though it is something they all share. Each of the divine Persons/emanations is *not* either of the other two Persons: originating is *neither* producing *nor* being a sending forth, producing is *neither* originating *nor* being a sending forth, and being a sending forth is *neither* originating *nor* producing. Even if perfect being and perfect goodness necessarily converge in one simple and transcendent plenum, presumably they are real properties or factors of this plenum between which there is some difference in virtue of which one is *not* completely the same as the other.[7] In some sense the divine intellect is *not* the divine will; one divine idea in the divine intellect is *not* another divine

---

superexcellent goodness are instantiated by the Trinitarian divine being is aided by Jesus Christ's revelation of the divine personal properties of originating, producing, and being a sending forth.

7. Similarly, being equilateral and being equiangular necessarily converge in a perfect triangle but aren't the same property. Perhaps, as Scotus might say, the real difference between these properties in objects where they don't coexist (e.g., a rectangle) is merely a formal difference in a perfect triangle where they necessarily coexist. Yet it remains unclear how the fact that an entity possessing a property *formally not* the same as another property it possesses avoids the consequence that the entity in question has something to do with nonbeing *ontologically*—especially if a formal difference isn't merely conceptual.

idea; and so forth, through all the permutations of negativity obtaining among these manifold differences within the divine being. For any two divine differences, it would seem that one must possess some being not possessed by the other in virtue of which they are not the same but different. But then the divine being has something to do with nonbeing after all, and hence does not instantiate *pure being*. Correlatively, if being is communicated fully and equally throughout divinity (for example, the divine Persons are said to be "one in being"), then for any pair of divine differences one cannot possess some being not possessed by the other, in which case there would appear to be no differences whatsoever within the plenum of divine being that instantiates *pure being*. Either alternative is disastrous for the philosophical and theological system presented in *The Soul's Journey into God*.

Bonaventure's reflections on ecstatic contemplation may be seen in part as an attempt to come to terms with the problem of negativity in divinity. Bonaventure says that

> when finally in the sixth stage our mind reaches that point where it contemplates in the First and Supreme Principle and in the *mediator of God and men* [1 Tim 2:5], Jesus Christ, those things whose likenesses can in no way be found in creatures and which surpass all penetration by the human intellect, it now remains for our mind, by contemplating these things, to transcend and pass over not only this sense world but even itself.[8]

"Those things whose likenesses can in no way be found in creatures and which surpass all penetration by the hu-

8. Ibid., 111.

man intellect" are the Trinitarian Persons, who cannot be comprehended solely on the basis of our intellect but only through the revelation of the God-man. Once we have attained a Christocentric comprehension of the Trinity, we are capable of the further contemplation described by Pseudo-Dionysius the Areopagite in his *Mystical Theology* and quoted by Bonaventure:

> But you, my friend, concerning mystical visions, with your journey more firmly determined leave behind your senses and intellectual activities, sensible and invisible things, *all nonbeing and being*; and in this state of unknowing be restored, insofar as it is possible, to unity with him who is above all essence and knowledge.[9]

Mystical contemplation supposedly pertains to divinity as it lies beyond not only being but also nonbeing, suggesting that any negativity in divinity has nothing to do with nonbeing ontologically. Let us pursue this suggestion by trying to form some idea of what Bonaventure means by ecstatic contemplation.

In a striking passage Bonaventure compares ecstatic contemplation to being consumed by the dark fire of divine flames:

> But if you wish to know how these things come about, ask grace not instruction, desire not understanding, the groaning of prayer not diligent reading, the Spouse not the teacher, God not man, darkness not clarity, not light but the fire that to-

9. Quoted in ibid., 114–15, emphasis added. For a different translation of this passage, see Pseudo-Dionysius, *Mystical Theology* 135.

tally inflames and carries us into God by ecstatic
unctions and burning affections.[10]

Using fire as an image of ecstatic contemplation faces an obvious drawback. Fire is one of the natural vestiges (*vestigia*)
through which we can see God on the basis of the proof by exclusion we considered in chapter 2. Yet at the seventh stage of
the soul's journey, "We have, therefore, passed through these
six [previous] considerations," including the initial stage at
which "our mind has beheld God outside itself through his
vestiges."[11] Given that the non-intellectual activity of ecstatic
contemplation differs entirely from the previous intellectual
activity of seeing God through the mirror of fire and other
vestiges, it follows that any description of ecstatic contemplation in terms of fire is metaphorical at best.

Sometimes Bonaventure describes ecstatic contemplation as a kind of death:

> Whoever loves this death can see God because it is
> true beyond doubt that *man will not see me and live*
> [Exod 33:20] Let us, then, die and enter into the
> darkness; let us impose silence on our cares, our
> desires, and our imaginings.[12]

Bonaventure doesn't believe that ecstatic contemplation involves literally dying. He tells us that, "This was shown to
blessed Francis when in ecstatic contemplation on the height
of the mountain . . . there appeared to him a six-winged
Seraph fastened to a cross"[13] before Francis received the

10. Bonaventure, *Soul's Journey into God*, 115.
11. Ibid., 110–11.
12. Ibid., 116.
13. Ibid., 112.

stigmata. Clearly St. Francis lived on for some time after his vision on Mount La Verna. Elsewhere Bonaventure explains that ecstatic contemplation involves being "*as if* dead to the outer world"[14] of material things, as well as to the inner world of our cares, desires, and imaginings, "but experiencing, as far as possible in this wayfarer's state, what was said on the Cross to the thief who adhered to Christ; *Today you shall be with me in paradise* [Luke 23:43]."[15]

Nevertheless, Bonaventure's allusion to Exodus 33:20, a scripture often associated with the beatific vision of God's essence, might be taken to imply that ecstatic contemplation just is the beatific vision. The fact that ecstatic contemplation can be enjoyed by the soul prior to bodily death doesn't automatically preclude ecstatic contemplation from being the same as beatitude; Scholastic theologians hold that although no one can naturally see God in this life, God can and has miraculously bestowed the vision of His essence upon some individuals, like Moses, prior to their bodily death.[16] Does ecstatic contemplation consist in God's miraculously bestowing the vision of His essence upon contemplatives like St. Francis during their lives? No. The decisive consideration against identifying ecstatic contemplation with the beatific vision is that the latter is still an act of the intellect.[17] But if,

14. Ibid., emphasis added.

15. Ibid.

16. For example, see *Summa Theologiae* 1a, q.12, a.11, ad.2.

17. See *Summa Theologiae* 1a2ae, q.2, a.5, where Aquinas argues that beatitude is an act of the speculative intellect. A rival conception of beatitude as primarily an act of the will, such as perfectly satisfied love (*fruitio Dei*), would still require beatitude to include an intellectual component, since there must be some understanding in the intellect of whatever is an object of the will.

as Bonaventure and Pseudo-Dionysius insist, ecstatic contemplation requires leaving behind all intellectual activities and understanding, then ecstatic contemplation cannot be a beatific intellectual act miraculously bestowed in this life.

What is ecstatic contemplation according to Bonaventure? The question might be dismissed as misguided. Ecstatic contemplation is a state for which there is no adequate description. To appreciate what it is you must undergo it, whereupon there will be no need for any description because you will directly know what ecstatic contemplation is, in the way that someone who has never tasted an orange will know what oranges taste like only upon eating one for the first time. Until then, all the wayfarer can do is desire, hope, and pray to be blessed with ecstatic contemplation during her spiritual journey. Bonaventure himself says as much:

> This, however, is mystical and most secret which *no one knows except him who receives it* [Rev 2:17], no one receives except him who desires it, and no one desires except him who is inflamed in his very marrow by the fire of the Holy Spirit whom Christ sent into the world.[18]

That Bonaventure regards ecstatic contemplation as something we can not only desire but also hope for is evident from the following passage: "Whoever turns his face fully to the Mercy Seat and with faith, hope, and love, . . . such a one makes the Pasch, that is the Passover, with Christ . . . where he will taste *the hidden manna* [Rev 2:17]" of ecstatic contemplation.[19] And the counsel to pursue "the groaning of prayer not

18. Bonaventure, *Soul's Journey into God*, 113.
19. Ibid., 111–12.

diligent reading"[20] in preparation for ecstatic contemplation indicates that Bonaventure regards the latter as something for which we can pray.

Yet if anything, the problem now becomes even more acute. To desire, hope, and pray for a possible outcome, at least we must be able to form some positive idea of it, however nebulous. Otherwise, if all we can say about the outcome in question is what it is not, then so far there is no difference between the outcome and nothing in particular: "Not cognition of a external vestige, not cognition of an internal image, not an instantaneous grasp that *pure being* and *superexcellent goodness* are instantiated by the divine being, not an act of beatitude, not any intellectual act whatsoever" is as apt a description of nothing in particular as it is of ecstatic contemplation. But we can only desire, hope, or pray for something or other; we cannot desire, hope, and pray for nothing in particular. Therefore, unless something positive can be said about ecstatic contemplation, it makes no sense for anyone to desire, hope, and pray for ecstatic contemplation as a possible outcome of the spiritual path Bonaventure lays out before us. Like *Waiting for Godot*'s hapless Vladimir and Estragon, we seem to find ourselves in the impossible predicament of being asked to wait for someone or something that is indistinguishable from nothing at all.

Throughout our commentary we have seen how crucial points in his philosophical and theological system Bonaventure draws upon ideas of his intellectual predecessors. Aspects of Aristotelian epistemology and Platonic metaphysics figure prominently in his account of how God

20. Ibid., 115.

is reflected in the image of our sensory experiences, and he utilizes the Neoplatonic notion of emanating to develop his theology of the Trinity. He quotes extensively from a poem about ecstatic contemplation by Pseudo-Dionysius, another thinker who is deeply influenced by Neoplatonism. Thus it is natural to wonder whether Bonaventure has at his disposal Neoplatonic resources enabling him to navigate these difficult waters. I believe he does. Although much of what follows is highly speculative, a great beauty of a profound philosophical and theological treatise like Bonaventure's is precisely how it invites us to speculate in a manner that is consonant with what we have learned, that addresses the problems and objections we have encountered, and that teaches us what we wish to know insofar as it is possible for us to know it. For the moment let us leave off trying to form a positive idea of ecstatic contemplation as an *act* or a *state* of the contemplative's soul and focus instead on the purported *object* of such contemplation: the divine being as a pure plenum that includes negativity but no nonbeing.

Consider the differences within divinity as Bonaventure understands it: the divine essence, the divine Persons, perfect being, perfect goodness, the divine will, the divine intellect, the divine ideas in the divine intellect, and perhaps others. Each of these differences is an entity in the broad sense of "entity" applying to anything that has being. To take some nondivine examples: properties, relations, individuals, events, and states of affairs are all entities in the sense that is correct to say that they are rather than that they are not. Using medieval terminology, we may say that each entity possesses *unum* or unity in the sense of uniqueness. The property *rectangularity* is uniquely the property it is, not some other property or relation or any entity of another category. Similarly, the individual Socrates is uniquely the entity he is. *Unum* as uniqueness is not some further property shared by all entities but what medieval metaphysicians call a "transcendental" applying to each entity of every different category.[21]

One possible explanation of the uniqueness of an entity X is in terms of X's *contrariety*, according to which X's uniqueness consists in X's not being any other entity Y, Z, and so forth.[22] Setting aside the question of whether this view is philosophically defensible, immediately we can appreciate why it is not available to Bonaventure as an explanation of divine differences. If the uniqueness of a difference within the divine being consisted in its not being any of the other divine differences, it would then follow that the difference in question lacks some being and hence that there is something of nonbeing in divine being. By the metaphysical side of the Plenum Principle, the divine being would not instantiate *pure being*.

But perhaps there is an explanation of uniqueness other than in terms of contrariety. As an initial approximation, consider what Duns Scotus calls the "haecceity" (*haecceitas*) of an individual substance.[23] According to Scotus, a common nature such as *rational animal* is individuated as a particular being of that kind—e.g., Socrates—not, as Aquinas thinks, by signate matter (the spatiotemporal continuity of this flesh

21. See King, "Scotus on Metaphysics," especially 26–28 for a helpful discussion of the fairly sophisticated treatment of the transcendentals in Scotus's metaphysics, though questions remain.

22. This view of uniqueness is endorsed in Heidegger, *Duns Scotus's Theory of Categories* and attributed to Scotus.

23. See Noone, "Universals and Individuation," especially 118–21 and the references therein to relevant works by Scotus.

and these bones) but by a positive singularity or a primitive "thisness." As such, Socrates' haecceity differs from Plato's haecceity. Neither of these haecceities is itself a being or an entity. On the other hand, neither of them is pure nonbeing or merely nothing at all. A haecceity is more like the structural principle of an individual substance whereby it is that *individual* substance.[24] Since Socrates is the individual human he is by virtue of Socrates' "thisness," rather than by virtue of Socrates' not sharing in the being of any other individual human, Socrates' individuality has nothing to do with nonbeing but only with a positive singularity. Granted, Socrates' "thisness" is *not* Plato's "thisness." But since Plato's "thisness" is not itself a being, the non-identity of Socrates' "thisness" with Plato's doesn't entail that Socrates' "thisness" lacks some being it might have and thus partakes of nonbeing.

Again, setting aside the vexed question of whether Scotus's notion of haecceity is philosophically defensible, it cannot serve as an explanation of uniqueness in general. Haecceities are principles of individuation in the category of substance. Hence if a property like *rectangularity* were the unique property it is by virtue of a haecceity, then it would no longer be a property of individual substances but would be an individual substance itself. Or if each of the divine Persons were the unique Person it is by virtue of its own haecceity, then the three divine Persons would be three individual substances, with the consequence that there are three Gods rather than only one. Even so, compared to the notion of contrariety the notion of haecceity has the conceptual advantage of explaining at least the uniqueness of individual

24. On one interpretation, Aristotelian actuality and potentiality are structural principles of being, not beings themselves.

substances without depriving any substance of some being; as a structural principle of uniqueness rather than a unique being itself, the "thisness" of one substance isn't some being lacked by all other individual substances. Similarly, if a *suppositum* is a structural principle of uniqueness in the category of persons rather than a particular "existence" or being itself, then (despite the difficulties with Scotus's notion of *supposita* mentioned in chapter 7) at least a person's uniqueness as determined by her *suppositum* isn't some being lacked by all other persons.

Haecceities and *supposita* can be designated as "sub-essential" and "sub-eminent" principles of uniqueness. For at best they only account for uniqueness in a given category—haecceities account for the uniqueness of substances, *supposita* account for the uniqueness of persons—not for the uniqueness of other entities such as properties and relations. A metaphysician might postulate sets of uniqueness principles corresponding to each category of entity: as many haecceities as there are unique substances, as many *supposita* as there are unique persons, as many "properticities" as there are unique properties, as many "relationicities" as there are unique relations, and so forth. Apart from being alarmingly non-parsimonious, the resulting plethora of principles doesn't really account for uniqueness, since all we know about the principle P for a given unique entity X is that P is related to X's uniqueness, not how P is related to it.

Alternatively, a satisfactory "super-essential" and "super-eminent" principle of uniqueness would account for the uniqueness of each entity in every category. There would be only one such principle operating from the "top down" so to speak, not a plethora of sub-principles operating from the "bottom up." Does Bonaventure countenance any super-essential and super-eminent principle of uniqueness along these lines? The first part of the entire passage he quotes from Pseudo-Dionysius is highly suggestive:

> Trinity, supper-essential, super-divine, and super-eminent overseer of the divine wisdom of Christians, direct us into the super-unknown, super-luminous and most sublime summit of mystical communication. There new, absolute and unchangeable mysteries of theology are hidden in the super-luminous darkness of a silence teaching secretly in the utmost obscurity which is super-manifest—a darkness which is super-resplendent and in which everything shines forth and which fills to overflowing invisible intellects with the splendors of invisible goods that surpass all good.[25]

The language of what "fills to overflowing invisible intellects" such as ours once we leave behind "sensible and invisible things, all being and nonbeing"[26] (115) is the language of the Neoplatonic One identified by Plotinus, Proclus, and Porphyry as neither a being nor nonbeing but as the principle of all uniqueness and the source of all being in the universe. We wish to discover whether Bonaventure can adapt the notion of the One as a super-essential and super-eminent principle of uniqueness within the divine being that neither explains divine differences by recourse to any nonbeing nor erases these differences altogether.

25. Quoted in Bonaventure, *Soul's Journey into God*, 114. For a different translation of this passage, see Pseudo-Dionysius, *Mystical Theology* 135.

26. Bonaventure, *Soul's Journey into God*, 115.

We might conceive of the One as a super-determinable that virtually includes as determinates each and every possible instance of uniqueness. To work our way toward this conception, we begin with a couple of examples. *Color* is a determinable that virtually includes as determinates *yellow*, *red*, *blue*, *green*, and every other possible color having nothing in common except that they are all colors.[27] Although *blue* lacks some being possessed by another color, such as the lightness of *yellow*, this deficit of being doesn't prevent *blue* from being as distinct a property as *yellow* is or from being as equally a color as *yellow* is. Hence the basis for each color being distinct isn't nonbeing or contrariety but merely the virtual inclusion of the determinate within the determinable *color*. Another, more metaphysical example is the quasi-determinable *humanity* that virtually includes as quasi-determinates Socrateity, Platoneity, Xanthippeity, you, me, and every other possible singular humanity.[28] Although Socrateity lacks being possessed by Platoneity, such as the latter's larger size, nonetheless Socrateity is as distinct a determinate as Platoneity and shares as equally as the latter does in being human, understood as the property of being some singular humanity or other. Hence again, the basis for each humanity's being a distinct determinate isn't nonbeing or contrariety but the

27. See Johnson, *Logic*, Part I for the classic discussion of determinable and determinates. More discussion and additional references can be found in the Sanford, Determinates vs. Determinables."

28. I use "quasi-determinable" and "quasi-determinates" to describe *humanity* and its instances of singular humanity because, unlike a pure determinable and determinates within it, singular humanities have it in common that they are all rational animals. This difference between a pure determinable/determinates within it and a quasi-determinable/ quasi-determinates within it doesn't matter for our present purposes.

virtual inclusion of the determinate within the determinable *humanity*.

We now move from these examples to the One, or "Oneness," as a super-essential and super-eminent determinable that virtually includes as determinates each and every instance of uniqueness: divine or non-divine, actual or non-actual, possible or impossible. In addition to the unique differences within divine being—a unique divine essence, a unique divine Father, a unique divine Son, a unique divine Spirit, a unique plenum of pure being, a unique superexcellent goodness, a unique divine idea of azure, a unique divine idea of Plato, and so forth—Oneness virtually includes among it determinates unique properties such as *rectangularity*, unique humanities such as *Xanthippeity*, unique non-actual possibilities such as *Socrates' being born in Sparta*, and even unique impossibilities such as *my desk being both round and square simultaneously* or *2+7=8*. Any two non-actual possibilities or impossibilities are just as distinctively unique as any two instances of actual uniqueness are, so that the basis of uniqueness isn't being or nonbeing but virtual inclusion within the determinable Oneness. In particular, then, the uniqueness of any divine difference X as opposed to the uniqueness of any other divine difference Y isn't that one difference lacks some being the other difference has but that both differences are determinates within Oneness as determinable. Furthermore, just as all distinct colors share equally in being a color and all singular humanities share equally in being human, so all unique differences within divinity share equally in divine being—not as a property, but as a plenum of necessary being in which there is no nonbeing whatsoever. Because the foregoing considerations subtract being and non-being from an explanation of determinate colors, determinate humanities, and determinate divine differences, we shall refer to them as *the argument by subtraction.*

Plotinus, Proclus, and Porphyry all conceive the One not only as the principle of all uniqueness but also as the source or cause of all being in the universe, yet not as a being itself. The idea of a "source" or "cause" that isn't a being is extremely counterintuitive. Here Bonaventure might adapt Neoplatonic views to his own purposes by dropping the idea that the One is a source or cause while retaining Oneness as a super-essential and super-eminent determinable principle of all uniqueness that isn't a being itself. Thus Oneness is neither "a God beyond God" nor the cause of any being, not even of its own determinates since a determinable doesn't cause its own determinates to be—especially not unique, non-actual possibilities which never will be, or unique impossibilities which can't be! Rather, all actual contingent being is creatively caused, sustained, and concurred with by the necessary divine being. All possibility or impossibility is reflected by the presence or absence of ideas in the divine intellect that itself shares in necessary divine being, making these possibilities and impossibilities necessarily possible or impossible. Oneness is simply that by virtue of which each and every determinate X is unique by virtue of its virtual inclusion in this super-essential and super-eminent determinable.[29] Postulating a single over-

29. An ordinary determinable such as *color* is associated with certain modal truths—e.g., necessarily redness is a color. Is the determinable Oneness also associated with modal truths—e.g., necessarily the divine essence is unique? As I interpret Bonaventure, his answer is no. Possibility applies only to actual being and to nonbeing that might be, not to nonbeing that cannot be. Necessity applies only to actual being that must be and, as impossibility, to nonbeing that cannot be, not to

arching principle of uniqueness is certainly more parsimonious than postulating a plethora of haecceities, *supposita*, and other sub-principles of uniqueness. Finally, our understanding of virtual inclusion of determinates within a determinable affords us some understanding of the relation between each instance of uniqueness and its principle of uniqueness.

Suppose that the argument by subtraction provides Bonaventure with an account of differences within divinity without introducing any nonbeing into divine being. What then of ecstatic contemplation as an act or state of the human soul? A seeker who has completed the penultimate stage of Bonaventure's spiritual itinerary grasps in an instantaneous cognition that both *pure being* and *superexcellent goodness* are instantiated by the divine being. Hence she has attained the summit of human conceptual achievement. And yet the seeker can also have some vague inkling of a broader principle of uniqueness encompassing each instance of divine uniqueness she has now conceptualized.[30] She need not describe the

---

actual being that might not be or to nonbeing that might be. (Necessity also applies to the possibility, impossibility, or necessity of any X.) Yet as a principle of uniqueness, Oneness applies to all being and nonbeing: actual being that must be, actual being that might not be, nonbeing that might be, and nonbeing that cannot be. (We also know that X is a unique something independently of knowing whether X is possible, impossible, or necessary, and hence also independently of knowing whether X is necessarily possible, necessarily impossible, or necessarily necessary.) Since each modal category is restricted within being and nonbeing whereas Oneness is not, Oneness exceeds modal categories. Perhaps this is another sense in which Oneness is "super-essential."

30. For those who don't share Bonaventure's conviction about what constitutes the summit of human intellectual achievement, it still seems plausible that upon reaching the limits of our current conceptualization we can still have an inkling of a broader unity encompassing what we have conceptualized. For example, subatomic particles, strings,

inkling she has as a notion of the determinable Oneness in which each and every uniqueness within divine being is virtually included as a determinate; nonetheless, Bonaventure or we might very well describe her inkling in these terms. Since the seeker's inkling of Oneness doesn't involve sensation, and since the seeker's inkling is also subsequent to what Bonaventure regards as the highest cognition of which any human intellect is capable primarily on its own, he would construe her inkling of Oneness as a non-sensory and non-conceptual state of the seeker's soul. Bonaventure might urge that when the seeker enters this state she begins to undergo ecstatic contemplation. Adapting the Neoplatonic One as the principle of all uniqueness neither is nor produces ecstatic contemplation by itself, but only enables us to form a positive idea of ecstatic contemplation as something we can desire, hope, and pray to undergo.

We round out this chapter with two queries which serve as our final set of discussion questions.

A mere inkling of the determinable Oneness that virtually includes as determinates every instance of uniqueness is an abstract, minimal, and tepid form of mental activity. It is devoid of any intense affection or ecstasy. The same certainly cannot be said of the mystical contemplation at the end of the soul's journey "that totally inflames and carries us into God by ecstatic unctions and burning affections."[31] Does this discrepancy count against our interpretation of ecstatic contemplation as having an inkling of the determinable Oneness? Or do we have here another case where Bonaventure can turn what

---

spatiotemporal dimensions, and fundamental forces are all determinate forms of physical uniqueness.

31. Bonaventure, *Soul's Journey into God*, 115.

looks like a liability for his position to his advantage? His seventh chapter heading describes mystical contemplation as that "in which rest is given to our intellect when through ecstasy our affection passes over entirely into God." Thus mystical contemplation involves the eventual transformation of some affection on the seeker's part into an ecstasy through which the seeker passes into God. Upon reaching the limits of human conceptualization, the seeker has an initial inkling of a broader Oneness encompassing each instance of divine uniqueness she has conceptualized. Although her initial inkling doesn't involve ecstasy, it may involve some affection or act of will on her part in the form of her curiosity to attain a clearer conception of Oneness. The more clearly you conceive a determinable, the more clearly you conceive each and every determinate virtually included within it. For example, the more clearly you conceive *color* or *humanity* the more clearly you conceive each and every color or each and every singular humanity virtually included within these respective (quasi-) determinables. Thus the more clearly the seeker conceives Oneness, the more clearly she conceives each and every instance of divine uniqueness virtually included within this determinable. Perhaps at some point her curiosity is transformed into unspeakable awe at what she is conceiving more and more clearly. This awe is spiritual ecstasy.

A potentially more worrisome question for Bonaventure is why a clearer conception of the determinable Oneness results in a clearer conception of the distinctively *divine* instances of uniqueness. After all, Oneness virtually includes as determinates all instances of uniqueness: divine or non-divine, actual or non-actual, possible or impossible. It would then seem that a clearer conception of the determin-

able would result in a clearer conception of uniqueness not
limited to the unique differences within divinity such as the
divine essence, the divine Persons, the divine intellect, the
divine will, divine pure being, divine superexcellent goodness, and divine ideas. However, if we read "super-essential
darkness" as a placeholder for the super-essential principle of
uniqueness that lies beyond our best conceptualization, then
plainly Bonaventure associates our more clearly conceiving
this principle not with our more clearly conceiving each and
every uniqueness per se but only with more clearly conceiving each and every divine uniqueness: "For transcending
yourself and all things, by the immeasurable and absolute
ecstasy of pure mind, leaving behind all things and freed
from all things you will ascend to the super-essential ray of
the divine darkness."[32] Unfortunately, Bonaventure offers no
clues as to how contemplation of the determinable Oneness
is focused exclusively on its divine determinates. He echoes
St. Paul's assurance in 1 Cor 2:10 that "this mystical wisdom
is revealed by the Holy Spirit"[33] without explaining how the
divine difference that is the Holy Spirit acts as the agent of
this revelation.

So we see that the conclusion of the soul's journey into
God is still haunted by the ghost of the Neoplatonic One extending not just to divine but all reality. Yet as a super-essential and super-eminent principle of uniqueness rather than
a medium for ecstatic contemplation of divine uniqueness,
Oneness remains a useful metaphysical tool. This matter, as
do the others we have discussed, merits further investigation.

32. Ibid.
33. Ibid., 113

The Pure Land

We have completed our study of *The Soul's Journey into God*. It remains to say something about how the present work relates to the spiritual journey St. Bonaventure describes.

Bonaventure's treatise is not the seven-stage ascent to God but only a blueprint of the ascent, supplemented with terse yet brilliant sketches of philosophical and theological material pertinent to each stage. In developing the Seraphic Doctor's sketches into lines of thought that the reader may wish to pursue, my commentary is twice removed from the spiritual journey. Thus we may wonder whether our study in these pages has *any* spiritual import.

The question is complicated by the fact that the intended audience for this book includes anyone—Catholic or non-Catholic, Christian or non-Christian, religious or non-religious—seeking a better understanding of Scholastic philosophical theology. If what has been said on Bonaventure's behalf in chapter 5 is true, then progress toward acquiring a better understanding of a philosophical and theological tradition isn't the same as progress in faith toward entering into a deeper relationship with God. As much as I would be pleased to learn that reading my commentary played a part in someone's conversion to the Catholic faith or in clarifying certain tenets of the Christian creed for a person who already professes them, my purpose here has not been to engage in homiletics or apologetics but to provide readers with the better understanding they seek.

If my objective hasn't been to win converts or refute opponents, then even less has it been to conduct a cunning rearguard action in the service of Christian orthodoxy designed to cast doubt on contemporary secular pieties. The result, I fear, would be the very Cartesian epistemological sterility, described and decried in chapter 1, of finding ourselves isolated on an island of endless skepticism, unable to budge in any direction. Readers began with their personal intuitions, beliefs, and desires—including, I hope, a desire to determine whether or not there are good reasons for or against the truth of what they and others who disagree with them believe. After having read what Bonaventure has to say and what I have to say about what he says, many if not most readers will probably retain their passionate convictions, their faith or lack of it, and their fundamental attitudes about what makes sense and what doesn't. So in spiritual terms, what if anything has changed?

I have tried to imbue my commentary with the same spirit I detect in Bonaventure's great treatise. That spirit isn't a doctrinal commitment but a sensibility combining patient inquiry, non-contentiousness, humility before ideas and arguments which may be extremely difficult to fathom initially, trust in one's own ability to make headway in interpreting and evaluating them, trust in others' ability to provide guidance by means of their own writings and dialogue, and peaceful assurance that through the consummation of labor a worthwhile whole will emerge in the fullness of time. Certainly Bonaventure's sensibility can be applied to any scholarly endeavor, not just to evaluating the specific philosophical and theological issues he engages. Yet philosophy and theology today are desperately in need of his sensibility, I believe. Bonaventure offers us a model of critical scholarship in these areas that is painstaking but not pedantic, broad but not shallow, committed but not inflexible, challenging but not obscurantist. It pursues the life of the mind not as a war of words or as transactions in a marketplace of ideas but as a pilgrimage, sometimes solitary, sometimes in the company of others, but always toward truth.

Pilate asked "What is truth?" We leave for another time the question of whether there is any ultimate truth worth discovering and instead ask, "What is worthwhile in the whole now before us?" In scholarly terms, the writer's work is worthwhile if it meets professional standards of clarity and rigor while facilitating the reader's comprehension of its subject matter. That assessment is for others to make. The collaborative work between this writer and his readers may also be worthwhile by encouraging us all to cultivate the calm spirit of intellectual pilgrimage in contexts besides the immediate one of Bonaventure's philosophical theology. However, there is another way our study might be worthwhile depending on how we go forth from Bonaventure's philosophical and theological edifice.

Much of that edifice bristles with unusual conceptions and dizzying perspectives that constitute a strange mix of the familiar and the alien. Encountering it is like entering a vast Gothic cathedral or visiting a distant country for the first time. We recognize the cathedral as a building, but its cornices, flying buttresses, and gargoyles are not our architecture; we recognize the hills, valleys, and forests of the country, but they are not our geography. Because of this oddness, when we leave the cathedral or depart the country and return home, our own buildings and landscape themselves look somehow different. Near the end of the *Phaedo*, Socrates describes a "pure land" above the surface of the earth on which we dwell:

> And in this fair region everything that grows—
> trees, and flowers, and fruits—are in a like degree
> fairer than any here; and there are hills, having
> stones in them in a like degree smoother, and more
> transparent, and fairer in color than our highly-
> valued emeralds and sardonyxes and jaspers, and
> other gems, which are but minute fragments of
> them: for there all the stones are like our precious
> stones, and fairer still.[1]

Let us think of the pure land, not as a more pristine earth or as an otherworldly realm where perfect Forms reside, but as the earth we all walk and the world we all inhabit—only now freshly seen after we have encountered something as markedly different as Bonaventure's outlook.

The freshness we may detect in the wake of our study is exciting and invigorating and might spur us to do any number of unexpected things: to study more writings by Bonaventure

---

1. Plato, *Phaedo*, 109.

or other Scholastics, to view medieval paintings or listen to medieval music, to commune more with nature, to read more widely, to compose poetry, to seek out old friends or cultivate new ones, to jot down ideas we've been mulling over for some time and share them with others, to take up a challenge we previously thought irrelevant, to abandon a challenge we previously thought unavoidable. For some, the fresh prospect of the pure land might throw an experience from the past into bold relief. For others, some hitherto unanticipated future possibility might become evident. There is no way of knowing in advance how our engagement with the freshness will turn out or what it will bring. Yet a new ray enters our vision, a kind of faith. A confident and patient expectation of eventual culmination takes hold, a kind of hope. An eager and even joyful involvement intertwines us with what is unfolding, a kind of charity.

The freshness of the pure land reminds me of an early spring morning over thirty years ago. I was sitting on the curb in front of my parents' house. The trees were bereft of leaves and unblessed with buds. It had rained the night before, leaving a tang of ozone in the air. Flesh-colored earthworms wriggled across the damp pavement toward the safety of grass. Beside the road was a pasture that plunged into a deep swale before rising to meet a patch of woods on the other side. A path led through the woods to a house where an old woman had lived alone for many years. From the top of the path you could see beyond her house to a meadow, a few rickety sheds, and in the distance a sagging barn with stables inside. I'd seen them all before but had no interest in seeing them again. It was Saturday and I was terminally bored. The sky was bland like soap, the sunlight so weak that objects cast the barest of shadows. But it was quiet enough to hear the snap of a twig fifty yards away.

There was a crackle of static as someone on the far side of the old woman's property began chanting into a microphone: louder, then softer, then louder again. I got up and made my way across the swale to the path to find out what was going on.

A forest of furniture—mahogany chairs, stools, benches, bookcases, a table, a desk—had sprouted beside the barn. The pieces sat on a large transparent plastic sheet stretched out in the meadow and held down at each corner with a rock. People were milling around as an auctioneer on a platform pointed at items and cajoled bids. Every so often a hand fluttered above the crowd. The auctioneer droned on and on, his amplified words blurring into their own echoes in the wan day. My ears were lulled and my gaze drifted to the ghostly blue range of mountains in the east. On nights when the farmers burned their fields to enrich the soil, the lower slopes glowed like foxfire.

Then in an instant that wasn't really an instant but the beginning of forever, it happened. As precisely as a butterfly pinned to a board, the woods, the mountains, the sky, the old woman, the people, life, death, the unseen horses in the barn down to the very hairs on their hides, and myself were all *placed*. The placing wasn't cruel but loving, a measuring Love more expansive that anything, yet as simple and palpable as fellowship at table with dear friends. From beyond it all the Love gave it all, enfolded it all, and guided it all back to the Love itself so that every trickle and every tear would eventually find its ocean. I had spent many previous Saturdays hiking or bicycling for miles, searching for something—only to return home disappointed at not finding it and dispirited at not knowing what it was I sought. Now, on the day of its choosing it had found me. It knew me. I knew it. And I wanted never to leave it.

Somehow, in the wake of Bonaventure's treatise, I find that I can say a little more about what I have never before been able to say: When I take the Host into my hands, I hold the Love that is always holding me. Now is then, then is now, and nothing has really changed. And I pray that someday, when the worries of this life cease, I can stay there and never leave it. *Soli Deo Gloria.*

What will you find yourself able to say or to do or to be?

Glossary

Ad extra: A term applying to anything external to the divine essence/divine being. For example, the universe and all the creatures it contains are *ad extra*.

Argument by subtraction: A form of reasoning that subtracts some condition from an explanation of why a range of instances are all determinates within a given determinable. For example, although *yellow* lacks some being possessed by another color, such as the saturation of *red*, *yellow* and *red* are equally colors, so that the basis of their being distinct determinates within the determinable color isn't *yellow*'s non-being relative to *red*. Thus the condition of non-being is subtracted from an explanation of determinate colors. Bonaventure may be interpreted as subtracting both being and non-being from an explanation of the determinate instances of uniqueness within the determinable Oneness, since all these determinates are equally unique though some lack being (e.g., the unique non-actual possibility of Socrates' being born in Sparta) while others have being (e.g., the unique property of rectangularity).

Being a sending forth: The divine relational property of being secondarily emanated without secondarily emanating a divine emanation. Bonaventure identifies this relation with the divine Person of the Holy Spirit.

Contrariety: An explanation of the uniqueness of an entity X, according to which X's uniqueness consist in X's not being any other entity Y, Z, and so forth.

Determinable/Determinates: A determinable is a concept or property with instances having nothing in common except that they are all examples of the determinable. *Color* is a determinable with the instances *yellow*, *red*, *blue*, and *green* having nothing in common except that they are all colors. By contrast, the instances of a non-determinable concept or property such as *squareness* are all four-sided, equilateral, and equiangular. The instances of a determinable are determinates of it. A determinable includes determinates not literally but virtually, in the way that a concept like *human* includes its differentiae *rational* and *animal*.

Divine relational property: A property something divine has only if it is primarily emanated and either secondarily emanates or is secondarily emanated by something else. The godhead or divine essence has no divine relational properties, though any emanation has some divine relational property that individuates it from the other emanations.

Emanation: A complete manifestation or full expression of divine being. Bonaventure identifies the three Persons of the Trinity as emanations which are one in being with the divine being that instantiates both *pure being* and *superexcellent goodness.*

First Principle: A being that is transcendent because it is not something in the universe and that possesses as an attribute the triple property of power, wisdom, and goodness encompassing every kind of power, wisdom, and goodness exhibited by beings in the universe.

Full analysis (*plene resolvens*): Either a definition containing the most basic notions involved in a complete understanding of the defined term (e.g., the definition of *human* as *rational, living, corporeal being*); or a proof by exclusion from things in the universe exhibiting some property to something not in universe exhibiting the same property. Both readings are possible interpretations of what Bonaventure means by *plene resolvens*, though his arguments are more plausible under the second interpretation.

Haecceity: The primitive "thisness" that is neither a being nor nonbeing but the positive singularity or structural principle in virtue of an individual substance whereby it is individual. For example, Socrates and Plato are distinct individual humans in virtue of their respective haecceities. Duns Scotus postulates haecceities to explain the uniqueness of substances.

Image (*imago*): Something in the universe that literally depicts God or an aspect of God. We see God "in the mirror" of His images. Bonaventure maintains that our sensory activities are images of God because are informed by divine ideas whenever we perceive external objects.

In extra: A term applying to anything that is internal to the divine essence/divine being. For example, the three Persons of the Trinity are *in extra*.

Likeness (*similitudo*): A special kind of image resulting when an intelligent creature is reformed by grace so that it resembles God as fully as it can. According to Bonaventure, through the operation of faith, hope, and charity the human soul becomes a likeness because its acts are fully integrated into divine order and it is directly aware of God and other spiritual realities.

Limiting situation: A situation in which there is no universe whatsoever, including no material things, no intelligent beings, no space, and no time.

Non-Nullity Principle: The principle that nonbeing depends both conceptually and ontologically on being. Bonaventure suggests that if *pure being* isn't instantiated then a state of total nothingness can obtain. But a state of total nothingness cannot obtain without a definite set of modal circumstances obtaining. Moreover, a state of total nothingness is compatible with different sets of modal circumstances. Thus there must be some being in virtue of which a definite set of modal circumstances obtains in a state of total nothingness. Hence a state of total nothingness cannot obtain without some being, in which case there cannot be a state of total nothingness and any nonbeing that obtains always depends on some being.

Oneness: A determinable that virtually includes as determinates unique properties, unique particulars, unique persons, unique possibilities, unique impossibilities, and every instance of uniqueness whether divine or non-divine, actual or non-actual, possible or impossible having nothing in common except that they are all unique. Since Oneness extends even to instances of uniqueness lacking being, Oneness is a metaphysical principle beyond being and non-being.

Originating: The divine relational property of secondarily emanating a divine emanation without being secondarily emanated itself. Bonaventure identifies this relation with the divine Person of the Father.

Plenum Principle: The principle that the concept *pure being* has nothing to do with nonbeing either conceptually or in our overall estimation of it and that anything instantiating *pure being* has nothing to do with nonbeing ontologically. The Plenum Principle plays a central role in Bonaventure's argument that *pure being* is instantiated by divine being.

Possibility Principle: The principle that the logical possibility of an external object with a property P consists in P's existing in a mode that is ontologically neutral between existing merely in the mind of some intelligent being in the universe and actually existing in an external object.

Primary emanating: The emanating of all emanations by the godhead. Bonaventure takes all three divine Persons to be primary emanations of the godhead, which is the divine essence.

Primary name of God (*primum nomen Dei*): A concept that that enables us to know God not through His vestiges or on the basis of His images but through intellectual contemplation. Bonaventure distinguishes two primary names of God: *pure being* and *superexcellent goodness.*

Producing: The divine relational property of secondarily emanating a divine emanation and being secondarily emanated itself. Bonaventure identifies this relation with the divine Person of the Son.

Proof by constructive elimination: An argument that considers a situation in which some condition obtains but in which many other factors are eliminated in order to construct a plausible explanation for that condition. Bonaventure may be interpreted as giving a proof by constructive elimination that considers the co-possibility of external objects possessing incompatible sensory properties in the limiting situation where there are no human minds containing ideas of these properties and then explains the co-possibility in terms of a divine mind containing ideas of them.

Proof by exclusion: An argument from the premise that things in the universe exhibit a property P to the conclusion that P is an attribute of something not in the universe. Bonaventure may be interpreted as giving a proof by exclusion from the premise that material things in the universe exhibit the triple property of power, wisdom and goodness by exhibiting trans-categorical characteristics, none of which are identical with the triple property, to the conclusion that the triple property is an attribute of a transcendent First Principle not in the universe. The Seraphic Doctor may also be interpreted as giving a proof by exclusion for the existence of transcendent and threefold necessity based on the necessity of axioms, inference rules, and conclusions.

Secondary emanating: The emanating of a divine emanation by some other divine emanation(s). Bonaventure takes the divine Person of the Son to be a secondary emanation of the divine Person of the Father, and the divine Person of the Spirit to be a secondary emanation of the Father and the Son.

Singular humanity: The metaphysically distinct humanities of individual human beings as opposed to their shared humanity. On this view, though human nature is metaphysically common to Socrates, Plato, and Xanthippe, their respective singular humanities—Socrateity, Platoneity, and Xanthippeity—are metaphysically distinct. The common *humanity* may be regarded as a quasi-determinable virtually including all possible singular humanities as quasi-determinates, since unlike a pure determinable and its determinates these instances are all rational animals.

Suppositum: The positive, non-relational existence that is neither a being nor a nonbeing but the structural principle whereby a person is that unique person rather than some other person. Duns Scotus postulates *supposita* to explain the ontological distinctness of the divine Persons as three *supposita* within the same divine essence.

Vestige (*vestigio*): Something in the universe that indicates the existence of a transcendent God without literally depicting either Him or some aspect of divinity. We see God "through the mirror" of His vestiges. More precisely, something is a vestige if it exhibits a property the full analysis of which leads to an attribute possessed by the First Principle.

Bibliography

Abelard, et al. *Five Texts on the Mediaeval Problem of Universals: Porphyry, Boethius, Abelard, Duns Scotus, Ockham*. Translated by Paul Vincent Spade. Indianapolis: Hackett, 1994.

Anselm of Canterbury. *The Major Works*. Edited by Brian Davis and G. R. Evans. Oxford: Oxford University Press, 1998.

Aristotle. *De anima*. Translated by H. Tancred-Lawson. Hamondsworth: Penguin, 1986.

Aquinas, Saint Thomas. *Summa Theologiae* 1a, q.27–q53 ("The Blessed Trinity"). Translated by Fathers of the English Dominican Province. New York: Benziger Bros., 1948. Online: http://www.newadvent .org/summa/1.htm.

Armstrong, D. M. *Universals: An Opinionated Introduction*. Boulder: Westview, 1989.

Augustine, Saint. *The City of God Against the Pagans*. Translated by R.W. Dyson. Cambridge: Cambridge University Press, 1998.

Austin, J. L. *How to Do Things with Words*. Oxford: Oxford University Press, 1976.

Bonaventure, Saint. *Commentaries on the Four Books of Sentences of Peter Lombard*, d. 24, pars 1, art 2, q. 4, 567–571. Translated by Br. Alexis Bugnolo. Online: http://www.franciscan-archive.org/bonaventura/ opera/bon02567.htm.

Bonaventure, Saint. *Itinerarium mentis in Deum*. In *Opera omnia S. Bonaventure.*, vol. V. Florence: Quaracchi, 1891, 295–316. Translated by Br. Alexis Bugnolo. Online: http://www.franciscan-archive.org/ bonaventura/opera/bon05295.html.

Bonaventure, Saint. *The Soul's Journey into God, The Tree of Life, and The Life of St. Francis*. Trans. Ewert Cousins. Mahwah, New Jersey: Paulist, 1978.

Bonaventure, Saint. *Works of St. Bonaventure: Breviloquium.* Edited by Dominic V. Monti, O.F.M. Saint Bonaventure University: The Franciscan Institute, 2005.

Cajetan, Cardinal Thomas. *The Analogy of Names and the Concept of Being.* Trans. Edward A. Bushinski, C.S.SP. Pittsburg: Duquesne University Press, 1953.

Carroll, Lewis. "What Achilles Said to the Tortoise." In *Mind* 4 (1895) 278–280. Online: http://www.lewiscarroll.org/achilles.html.

Cross, Richard. "Duns Scotus on Divine Substance and the Trinity." *Medieval Philosophy and Theology* 11 (2003) 181–201.

Dean, Fr. Maximilian Mary, FI. *A Primer on the Absolute Primacy of Christ: Blessed John Duns Scotus and the Franciscan Thesis.* New Bedford: Academy of the Immaculate, 2006.

Descartes, René. *The Philosophical Writings of Descartes: Volume 2.* Translated by John Cottingham, Robert Stoothoff, and Dugald Murdoch. Cambridge: Cambridge University Press, 1985.

Dillard, Peter S. *Heidegger and Philosophical Atheology: A Neo-Scholastic Critique.* London: Continuum, 2008.

———. "A Minor Matter? The Franciscan Thesis and Philosophical Theology." In *The Heythrop Journal* 50 (2009) 890–900.

Fodor, Jerry A. and LePore. Ernest. *Holism: A Shopper's Guide.* Cambridge: Blackwell, 2004.

Heidegger, Martin. *Duns Scotus's Theory of the Categories and of Meaning.* Translated by Harold Robbins. Chicago: DePaul University Press, 1978.

House, Adrian. *Francis of Assisi: A Revolutionary Life.* Mahwah, New Jersey: HiddenSpring, 2001.

Husserl, Edmund Husserl. *Cartesian Meditations: An Introduction to Phenomenology.* Translated by Dorion Cairns. New York: Springer, 2008.

Johnson, W.E. *Logic*, Part I. Cambridge: Cambridge University Press, 1921.

King, Peter. "Scotus on Metaphysics." In *The Cambridge Companion to Duns Scotus.* Edited by Thomas Williams, 15–68. Cambridge: Cambridge University Press, 2003.

Kripke, Saul. *Naming and Necessity.* Cambridge: Harvard University Press, 1980.

Lewis, David K. *Counterfactuals.* Oxford: Blackwell, 1973.

Lewis, David K. *On the Plurality of Worlds.* Oxford: Blackwell, 1986.

Noone, Timothy B. "Universals and Individuation." In *The Cambridge Companion to Duns Scotus*, Edited by Thomas Williams, 100–128. Cambridge: Cambridge University Press, 2003.

Malcolm, John. *Plato on Self-Predication of Forms: Early and Middle Dialogues*. Oxford: Clarendon, 1991.

Oppy, Graham. "Ontological Arguments." Stanford Encyclopedia of Philosophy (2007). Online: http://plato.stanford.edu/entries/ontological-arguments/.

Paley, William. *Natural Theology*. Oxford: Oxford University Press, 2008.

Plantinga, Alvin. *The Nature of Necessity*. Oxford: Oxford University Press, 1974.

Plato. *The Dialogues of Plato*. Translated by Benjamin Jowett. Oxford: Oxford University Press, 1892.

Plotinus: Volume VII, *Ennead* VI.6–9. Translated by A.H. Armstrong. Cambridge: Harvard University Press, Loeb Classical Library No. 468: 1988.

Pseudo-Dionysius the Areopagite. *The Complete Works*. Translated by Paul Rorem. Mahwah, New Jersey: Paulist, 1987.

Reichmann, Fr. James B., S.J. "Aquinas, Scotus, and the Christological Mystery: Why Christ Is Not a Human Person." *The Thomist* 71 (2007) 451–474.

Salmon, Wesley, editor. *Zeno's Paradoxes*. Indianapolis: Bobbs-Merrill, 1970.

Sanford, David. H. Stanford. "Determinates vs. Determinables." Stanford Encyclopedia of Philosophy (2006). Online: http://plato.stanford.edu/entries/determinate-determinables/#3.

Scotus, John Duns. *A Treatise on God as First Principle*. Translated by Allan B. Wolter, O.F.M. Chicago: Franciscan Herald, 1966.

Scotus, John Duns. *Ordinatio* 1, d. 3, q. 1. In *Duns Scotus: Philosophical Writings* ("Man's Natural Knowledge of God"). Translated by Allan B. Wollter, O.F.M. Indianapolis: Hackett, 1987, 13–33.

Shoemaker, Sydney. "Causality and properties." In *Identity, Cause, and Mind*, 206–233. Oxford: Oxford University Press, 2007.

Spinoza, Benedict de. *A Spinoza Reader: The* Ethics *and Other Works*. Translated and edited by Edwin Curley. Princeton: Princeton University Press, 1994.

Wittgenstein, Ludwig. *Philosophical Investigations*. Translated by G.E.M. Anscombe. Oxford: Blackwell, 1968.

Wolterstorff, Nicholas. *Divine Discourse: Philosophical Reflections on the Claim that God Speaks*. Cambridge: Cambridge University Press, 1995.

Index

A

acceptable argument, 79–80

activity, of things, 19–20

acts of obedience, required to be freely done, 95

actual being, God as total cause of, 122

ad extra, 189
- Jesus Christ, creating, 151
- three-in-one divine being, free acts, 152
- universe, creating, 133

analogous being (*esse analogum*), 113–14, 113n

analogy of inequality, 113n

Angelic Doctor (Aquinas), 102. *See also* Aquinas, St. Thomas

angelic hierarchy, nine-fold, 88n

angelic knowledge, depending on human sin, 150

angels
- comprehending Trinitarian Persons, 150
- described, 149
- different kinds of, 88n
- governing the universe, 93
- nine choirs of, 87
- power of, 89n

angles, hierarchically ordered, 89n

Anselm, St., "ontological argument," 108

Aquinas, St. Thomas. *See also* Angelic Doctor (Aquinas)
- beatitude as an act of the speculative intellect, 166a
- on Christ's assumed human nature, 156n
- essential attributes of intellect and will, 153
- operations appropriated to a specific Person, 153–54
- signate matter, 170–71
- *Summa Theologiae*, 146n

argument by subtraction, 176, 177, 189

Aristotelian epistemology
- aspects of, 32, 168–69
- Platonic metaphysical twist, 36
- sensory likenesses (*similitudines*), 33–34

Aristotle, 34n, 42

Austin, J. L., 96

Avicenna, 58n

awareness, distinction between direct and indirect, 101

awe, unspeakable, 179